FOUR KEYS TO
EL SALVADOR

by

Lilly de Jongh Osborne

FUNK & WAGNALLS COMPANY · NEW YORK

To my friends,
the people of El Salvador

1

PREFACE

In the following pages I have tried to present some of the many interesting things that can be told about El Salvador: its past, its present, and its most promising future.

Though much has been written about El Salvador in the Spanish language, so far there has been almost nothing in English about this remarkable country. I owe much to those well-informed writers in Spanish for that information I could not personally gather during my nine years in the country.

It is difficult, in the compass of this book, to discuss extensively the ancient Indian sites of this enchanting land. And it has been equally hard to do justice to the many outstanding writers, artists, musicians, and scholars of the El Salvador of today: all merit so much more than the passing word I have found it possible to offer them here. However I must gratefully mention Anibal Salazar, for it is he who took so many of the pictures that appear in this book. I wish also to express my gratitude to TACA, the Salvadorean airline, and to *Junta Nacional de Turismo* (the National Tourist Board) for their help in obtaining so many excellent illustrations.

Lilly de Jongh Osborne

v

CONTENTS

CONTENTS ix

Illustrations at page 84 *and page* 148.

INTRODUCTION

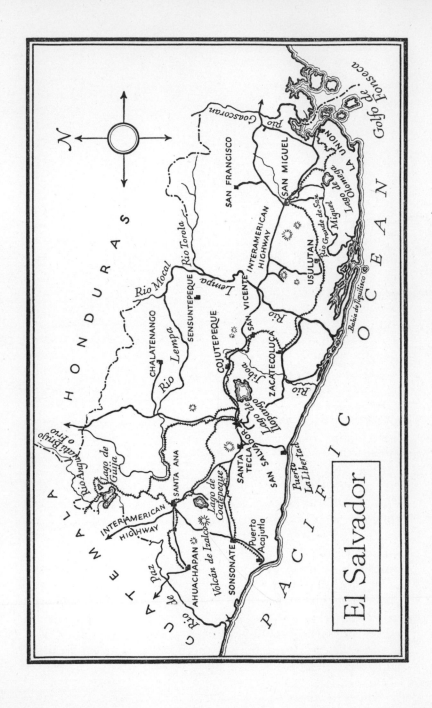

I

CUZCATLÁN—EL SALVADOR

EL SALVADOR is one of the most densely populated countries in the world and the smallest of five sister republics of Central America. It is the only one of the five having but one seaboard, the Pacific, and therefore is classed as one of the Pan-Pacific countries. The Indian name, Cuzcatlán, is still the one beloved of its inhabitants. To the outside world it is known as El Salvador, not to be confused with the island of San Salvador whereon Christopher Columbus set foot after his first perilous journey of discovery.

The boundaries of the Republic of El Salvador are: on the North and West the Republic of Guatemala; on the North and East the Republic of Honduras; on the South, the Pacific Ocean and the Bay of Fonseca, wherein are nine small islands that constitute the maritime territory of this country.

From time immemorial when Indian tribes crossed and recrossed this territory on their routes between North and South and between East and West, the country has been the crossroads of Central American migrations, a place of historic meetings and of amalgamations of different races.

The country is volcanic, therefore its configuration has constantly changed. Where lovely valleys extended some centuries ago offering luxuriant vegetation, now towering volcanoes intercept the horizon. Where brooks rippled and sang merrily on their way through quiet fields, now roaring rivers cascade down high cliffs into deep canyons on their way to the sea. Where formerly lush green vegetation soothed the sight, now great black lava fields extend for miles. Where

formerly placid pools and lakes contributed water to vegetation, now deep fissures mark the same spots and dry fields
surround the area where a seismic upheaval drank the precious liquid in thirsty gulps, leaving a barren soil.

The country we know as El Salvador is inseparably linked
with Central America. Historically it has the same three
well-defined periods: the pre-Columbian, from time immemorial to the Spanish conquest in 1524; the Colonial until
1821; and the Republican or independent period after the
latter date. However, this country has also a fourth and well-
marked period that ought to be added: the modern, meaning the last twenty-five years, wherein an amazing stride
forward has occurred in every activity and phase of life, and
which most emphatically must be taken into account as
perhaps its greatest historical period.

Though closely related to the other countries in Central
America, it can in no wise be compared to any of the others,
and must be considered from an entirely different viewpoint,
so as to understand the present country and its people. Each
historical period developed an individuality different from
its neighbors. First and foremost because of its climate, and
because of the physical qualities of its soil and the different
races that took root in its territory, this country emerges
with an individuality of its own, interesting and well worth
studying on its own merits.

PRE-COLUMBIAN ERA

II

THE INDIAN ANCESTORS

I T IS a daring venture to attempt to say who were the first inhabitants in the ever-changing kaleidoscope of scenery, as well as of humans, in what is now the Republic of El Salvador.

Nomad races lived in the lush forests, where hunting was rewarding and fish in the sea plentiful. They came from the north or from the south, stayed a while and disappeared, leaving no permanent trace of their presence. It is generally believed that a primitive people lived in caves, also in stone shelters, and when food grew scarce they migrated.[1]

Later known as Amerinds, they might have been the remnants of a Neolithic-age migration from the Orient. Descending the Pacific Coast of North America, some remained in this territory. Others continued southward. These early settlers may have been the discoverers of weaving when they first twisted vines and fibers into strands. Gradually they evolved weaving and made garments enough to provide covering for their bodies, leaving their hands free for the chase. These first garments served as protection against the insects so abundant in the forests.

With plentiful food and the warm climate the people multiplied, their bodies grew strong, and their needs were easily fulfilled. They worshiped the elements of Nature. Other races mingled with them, and the more advanced imposed their own cultures. They used clay implements, more or less crudely modeled, and made figurines of clay. Artifacts that

[1] Remains of enormous animals of thousands of years ago have been found in various parts of the country; evidently these are bones of animals unknown at the present time.

7

have been found all over this country are of a very early
type. In various sections—principally along the coast—are
carved stones, both large and small, as well as carvings on
walls of caves, whose significance has not been determined.
They may be vestiges of primitive cultures of races unknown
to us. However, petroglyphs have occurred in many pre-
Columbian sites belonging to the Arawak Indians in the
West Indies; other Caribbean Islands have petroglyphs that
might have belonged to some people of the Carib territory.
It is a mystery how, so far south as the Salvadorean territory,
the inhabitants—perhaps merchants—belonging to these island races may have gone.

At a very early stage of the history of El Salvador, the
Northern and Southern Indians discovered corn in the
northern hills—probably about 1000 B.C. The plant *teocentli*
(teosinte), closely related to *Zea mays* (maize or more commonly corn) was also growing in this rich soil, and these
Indians succeeded in acclimating and developing their own
species of corn. With this epoch-making event assuring the
food supply, and with knowledge of the bow and arrow add-
ing to it further, the Indians had leisure to initiate and develop arts and crafts.

THE MAYA INDIANS

These Indians contributed toward the early history of El
Salvador. Apparently several branches of this powerful race
established themselves in different regions at some time between the sixth and first century B.C. They developed their
particular civilization, but never reached the stage that has
been called "The Golden Age of the Maya"—from about
A.D. 500 to A.D. 731. To the north of this country at Copán
(Honduras), the Maya developed one of their greatest architectural centers, having structures with vaulted and arched
chambers, and tall stone stelae bearing on their four sides
hieroglyphs and carvings of events in their history. Though
this superartistic level does not seem to have been developed
in El Salvador, it is evident that a high Mayan culture ex-

isted in various sections of this country at a very early time, demonstrated by beautifully colored and engraved clay artifacts as well as ruins of temple mounds and village centers. However, the portable articles may easily have been trade wares.

The Maya were a peaceful people, as demonstrated by the carvings and inscriptions on the monuments; they depict religious ceremonies, and present dates without much reference to warfare. They achieved the highest intellectual plane on this continent; the knowledge of architecture, sculpture, ceramics, and cotton weaving was brought to a high degree of perfection; they developed ideographic writing and an astounding numerical system. The ruins of the Maya civilization that have been found in El Salvador seemingly belonged to a much earlier period than the ruins of the Maya to the North, associated with their highest artistic phase. They lived, and for causes unknown they vanished. One reason might have been the exhaustion of the soil for their crops; another, a possible revolt of the peasant class against their intolerable burden of work and the excessive cruelty of the ruling class.

No agricultural system as we understand it existed at that time. The Indians went out to the nearest forest, felled and burned the trees and underbrush, and so prepared the land for planting. A strong pointed stick was used to make holes in the ground, wherein the Indian planted a few grains of corn. The rains watered this virgin soil and fertilized the seed, and soon the earth was covered with a lush green carpet, a promise of enough food for the Indian. This *milpa* system originated at least three thousand years ago, and despite modern improvements in agricultural implements the present-day Indian still adheres to his old-style system: the best possible new soil in which to plant his next crop is sought, so as to leave the former one fallow until it once more is ready to produce its full quota of corn.

The principal Maya sites in this country were probably around what is now known as San Andrés, Tehuacan, Tazumal, and Cihuatan. These names were given by the Nahuatl Indians of a more recent time, though mounds and Maya artifacts have been found all over this country, wherever work has been carried out by scientists or erection of buildings has necessitated the excavation or removal of the old sites.

A prominent branch of the Maya, the Pokomám Indians, were also established in the western part of this country. The Pokomámes were influential in the latter part of the pre-Columbian epoch of the Cuzcatlán kingdom. Finding themselves much overcrowded and harassed by neighboring tribes, they solicited the Cakchiqueles in Guatemala to grant them lands on which to settle. This was done just before the Conquest and they settled on the plains between the Sacatepequez and Cakchiquel nations in Guatemala. A few remained in El Salvador and their descendants still inhabit the same sites as their forefathers, though in no wise have they preserved distinctive costumes or customs or even remnants of their former language. In certain sections of the country a ceremony was carried out a few years ago in accordance with the ritual *Tzolkin* calendar of 260 days, a characteristic Maya institution and a calendar evolved by those intellectual people.

Another later Maya-Quiché population settled in this country. Before the Conquest, Indians from the Kekchí region in Guatemala traded over well-known routes back and forth, principally with the region now comprised in the department of Sonsonate. They brought dyewood—*campeche*— and took back the balsam, indigo, cacao, and tobacco growing so abundantly in this rich soil. Finally many of the Kekchí Indians migrated and established themselves permanently so as to benefit from the natural wealth of the region. Another blood mixture took place and the stronger absorbed the lesser, so that at the present day hardly a vestige remains of this migration, unless it is the survival of one of their crafts, gourd decoration.

At the present time, it is believed that the inhabitants of the villages of Santiago, San Juan, and San Pedro Nonualco are descendants of the Maya, though nothing remains to demonstrate whether or not this is a fact. The word *Analco* or *Nonualco* is conceded to mean "where the language changes," or where the Nahuatl strain ended and another race of Indians had their sites.

THE LENCA INDIANS

The Lencas, also known as the Chorotegas, are supposed to be a distant and early branch of the Maya-Quiché Indians, particularly of those belonging to the Chorti family, numerous in Guatemala and Honduras. The Lencas belonged to the Kingdom of Chaparrestique to the west of the River Lempa. This was one of the most important groups of Indians in this country at the time of the Conquest. Their heroic last chief, the legendary Lempira, with his Indian hordes valiantly resisted the Spanish invasion. The ruins of the chief center of these people are not far from the present city of San Miguel. Many mounds and artifacts are scattered throughout the plains in this vicinity. The Lencas are generally considered to have been on a lower level of culture than the Indians of the rest of the country. Nevertheless, they had some degree of development and culture as proved by their ceramics, which are artistically colored and designed.

They had a written language that is still extant, and was spoken in the Lenca region about half a century ago. Historical accounts give meager information about these Indians. It is probable that most of them were absorbed eventually into the more powerful tribes that migrated from the north, that is to say, from the Mexican tablelands. The Lencas in their heyday spread rapidly, almost completely surrounding a small group of Matagalpa Indians, who had come to settle in this region near to what are now known as the towns of La Unión, Morazán, Cacaopera, and Lislique. The Matagalpa Indians are part of the great Chontal or Matagalpa group. The present village of Cacaopera is the largest site where the Matagalpa group at one time flourished.

Mexican Migrations

The Toltecs, a primitive Mexican race, migrated toward the south in the eleventh century and settled in what is now El Salvador. They spoke another language and their customs were very different from those of the people they found in these lands. Because of disturbances in their own country other Mexican groups, not necessarily of Toltec affiliation, left for the South. They found the lands of what is now El Salvador to their taste, so they overspread the greater part of the area, overcoming the earlier Indian inhabitants. They became known as the Nahoas or Nahuatl Indians and formed a powerful nation, the Cuzcatlán.

The Kingdom of Cuzcatlán was divided into *cacicazgos*— political divisions—ruled by a *cacique* or chief. The chief of Cuzcatlán was at the same time the ruling head of many smaller but no less important *cacicazgos*. The principal ones were the Izalcos, Ahuachapán, Apanhectl, Apaxtepetl, Ixtepetl, and Guacotechli, who formed a kind of federation known as the Cacicazgo of Cuzcatlán. This group was ruled with an iron hand by the chief. However, the Izalcos, though depending on the others, were of greater importance with a large territorial extension and a dense population. Their head group was called Tecuzalco.

It must be borne in mind that the Nahoas or Nahuatl, also known at the present time as the Pipiles, were not pre-Columbian migrants only; Indians from Mexico migrated southward after the Conquest, as disturbances forced them to seek new homelands. This time their migration was due especially to the treatment they received from the priests; thirty-two villages in southern Mexico revolted against the Spanish priests of the Order of Santo Domingo in the year 1712, but finally they were overcome. The Indians in this most recent migration arrived in the regions of what are now the departments of Sonsonate and San Salvador.

The name *Pipiles* is attached to those Indians who arrived as followers of the Spanish conquerors. The Mexican Indian soldiers found that the Indians belonging to the Nahuatl tribes, who had settled in days long past in the territory of Cuzcatlán, were able to understand their language. It was a Mexican language, but a language of a more educated people. It meant that the Cuzcatlán Indians had preserved their language throughout the period after they had left Mexico, as also they had preserved their religion, customs, dress, rites, and the background of their former homeland. They carried on the same agriculture—that is to say, corn; they planted maguey for their intoxicating ritual drink, using the fiber of this plant for weaving their garments. They lived from the chase, they ate the fish from the sea and rivers, supplying the needed vitamins with many chile peppers and herbs of different kinds. They knew the secret of extracting balsam. They pacified their deities with human offerings. They invoked the blessing of the deities on their corn crops by the sacrifice of a child in the summer solstice. Therefore, the pre-Columbian history of the Nahuatl Indians who settled in this country is that of their forefathers in the Mexican tablelands, with the modifications and variations developed by their acculturation with other tribes according to the section of the country concerned and the inhabitants they found therein.

To judge by the present-day descendants, these people were small, well formed, agile and healthy, dark skinned, with straight hair; they were very gifted in all kinds of useful crafts. They maintained a sporadic contact with their northern relations by commerce. They did not possess any codices (books painted on maguey or deerskin), and so their prehistoric era is known only through the traditions of the same race in the north.

However, the two Mexican calendars, *Tonalamatl* and *Tonalpouali*—the first consisting of 260 days, and the other of 360 days, with five additional days at the end—were well known by the Nahuatl Indians in this country. Even at the present time a few remnants of these calendars are preserved for use in certain rites in their religious ceremonies and in calculations for the time when corn should be planted.

Speaking of crops, in this fertile country there are some

sections where three crops of corn are planted every year. Nahuatl names designate them: *Tunamil (Maíz de sol—*sun corn), corn planted in the month of September, when the rainy season is about to end; *Supanmil (Maíz de invierno—*winter corn), corn planted either in April or May, when the rainy season starts; *Apanmil (Maíz de regadillo—*irrigated corn), planted at the end of December, and needing irrigation. Like all early Indians, the Nahoas employed the system of *milpas* for their agriculture.

They prospered and gradually absorbed the lesser tribes they found in other regions of the country. They imposed their culture and their language on the different sections wherein they settled. The Nahuatl Indian descendants now speak the best and purest language in such villages as Ushitlán, La Costa del Bálsamo, Tiutepec (Teotepeque), Chiltiupán, Shicalapa, Los Texacuangos, San Julián, sites on the mountain slopes or near the sea. In such villages as Izalco, Nahuazalco, Panchimalco, Aculhuaca, Paleca, Apastepeque, Ataco, and Tacuba, as well as in the small islands of Gubar and Faitza in the river Ahuachapán, though, the language is much more mixed.

The chief center of the Cuzcatlán kingdom at the time of the Conquest was built on a site that later was filled in by a lake. Subsequently, it again dried up (1873) as a result of volcanic action. It is now known as Antiguo Cuzcatlán (see page 172). The history of the various chiefs who ruled this nation is obscure. However, the oldest son inherited his father's throne with prior approval of the council. Women were not allowed to rule, but a girl was allowed to divide with her brothers the wealth left by her father. In current writings and in legends it is said that chiefs of the Cuzcatlán nation were legendary figures: there was the great Atlacatl, to whom a superman's powers have been attributed. However, the superman Atlacatl was possibly the last chief, and many have been with Atonal (*Sol de Agua—*Water Sun) the last heads of the Cuzcatlán nation, who confronted the Spaniards at the head of the Indian hordes. They may really have been generals who fought bravely to defend their lands, but unfortunately could not hold off the incoming avalanche of white men. Imprisoned, robbed of all their vast domains, the Indians finally came to a tragic end and with them ended the glory of the Cuzcatlán nation as an independent unit.

Different races of Indians followed in the train of Alvarado and his army. The greatest number were Tlascaltecas, who played an important part in the conquest of all these lands. A great many settled in this country and their descendants are found in such places as the village of Mejicanos, near the capital, and another Mejicanos near Sonsonate.

EARLY ARTIFACTS

The many upheavals associated with volcanic action in this country have scrambled and mixed the stratifications of the soil, so that side by side may be found vestiges of the earliest pre-Columbian races with those of the later arrivals, and side by side with the most ancient pottery has been found superlatively beautiful Maya ware. Everywhere remains have been disturbed, so that nothing precise can be maintained as to the date of the early migrations and the periods in which they developed their civilizations. It is even difficult definitely to specify the regions where this or that Indian race settled, except in those villages where the Indian descendants have preserved in a measure their traditions and languages, even though some acculturation has taken place in almost all of them.

Among the artifacts and different articles found among the ruins of early Indian sites, there are some that are typical. Although it is difficult to determine, because of the conditions mentioned above, the region to which these ceramics are indigenous, the only resource is to speak of the ceramics and other articles as coming from certain centers of interest to archaeologists and let each be studied individually.

Plumbate Ware—Until a few years ago, this ware was generally considered to be exclusively of this country, and more definitely to have its origin in the region of Suchitoto. Later studies have revealed that this plumbate ware is found in other localities in Central America, and therefore the local claim is no longer tenable. This peculiar ware appears in prettily shaped vessels having anthropomorphic and zoo-morphic figures, or in plain rounded effigy jars without handles. The color is a grayish glaze with deep orange, buff red, dark olive green, and gray. The glaze is over the basic clay, which gives it a characteristic color.

Plumbate ware is considered by some students to belong to the Totonac culture (Southern Mexico), mingled with that of the Pipil. The typical Tlaloc (Rain God) jar is more often found in regions where Nahuatl or Pipil settlements have occurred, or in regions where it is known that commerce was carried on with Pipil tribes.

The ware that has been named *Usulután* is also a disturbing element in the classification of archaeologists. It is named for the region in the department of Usulután wherein it has been found in great quantities. It is distinguished by its well molded, round shape whereon are light vertical lines that follow the contours. This decoration is made in the negative process (see page 92). Both the process and this particular kind of clay have been classified as of a very early date. In every corner of the country, wherever an excavation is undertaken or where plowing is carried on for agricultural purposes, prehistoric ceramics are unearthed. They are plentiful and of every kind: stone figures, clay jars, obsidian implements, jadeite amulets, plain and carved. From the highest art in the painted vessels to the plain unadorned clay pitchers, one and all are interesting, artistic, and intriguing, but it is a problem to speak definitely of their age or of the people who made them.[1, 2]

[1] The law prohibits exportation of any archaeological material.
[2] Interesting collections are at the National Museum; Dr. Emeterio Salazar, Dr. Orlando de Sola, Mr. Walter Soundy, and others in different parts of the country have worthwhile collections.

COLONIAL ERA

Despite the general opinion that one and all of the conquerors and Spanish settlers in this country were cruel and through their treatment of the Indians furthered their extinction, there are numerous *Cédulas Reales* (Royal Decrees), whereby His Majesty the King of Spain during the sixteenth and seventeenth centuries prohibited the mistreatment of Indians by the colonizers, and strictly circumscribed the various occupations. The King also prohibited Spaniards and Negroes from living together in the villages, a decree which was not always carried out. In fact, those decrees even established the number of Indians a Spaniard might take on trading journeys. The Spanish subject was obliged to state the number of Indians who were going with him and had to comply strictly in bringing them back. Also, Indians were prohibited from being taken to Spain, or being made slaves of *caciques* (chiefs) and other high-cast Indians, and it was forbidden that slaves should be taken from among Indians who had not been at war with the Spaniards. Most emphatic decrees were published in the early days of the sixteenth century about teaching the Indians the Spanish language, and at the same time urging the friars to learn the various Indian languages.

The kings were anxious to have information as to the appearance, customs, and general description of the new vassals under their jurisdiction, so that it should be said that the higher authorities in Spain tried their utmost to help the condition of the Indians. At the same time, the far-distant Spanish colonizers and religious orders paid scant attention to what was decreed in Spain. Nevertheless, the good intention was there, and must be stated, contrary to what is accepted as fact.

III

THE CONQUEST

WHEN Hernando Cortés left Spain in 1519, he brought out with him to the New World a young captain by the name of Pedro de Alvarado, handsome and blue-eyed, with fair hair and tawny beard, brave and cruel, with an unquenchable ambition to acquire wealth in the New World. Cortés was busy putting to rights his Mexican conquests, when he sent Alvarado in 1523 to conquer new lands farther south.

Arriving in what is now Guatemala, Alvarado encountered thousands of warlike Indians. At every step he and his followers were set upon by unknown dangers, variable climates, unknown wild beasts, and fearsome insects whose bite was poisonous. He and his army descended to blazing lowlands where they had to cross treacherous malarial swamps, deserts where neither food nor water was available, forests where every tree hid a menace, rivers that cost men and beasts their lives when they tried to ford the turbulent waters. Alvarado and his army climbed high mountains and shivered in the blasts of icy winds. There was no end to the dangers that confronted this courageous young man at the head of his army of white men with a handful of Tlascala and Cholula Indian allies. Their greatest boon was their horses, before which the Indians drew back in awe.

Alvarado was fortunate and conquered vast lands in the name of the Crown and Cross, "that I might receive both mundane and heavenly favors." Having established his first headquarters in Guatemala in 1524, he prepared for an expedition still farther south, ambitious for new lands to conquer, and avaricious for gold and treasure. Followed by his

19

Mexican allies and faithful Spaniards, Alvarado subdued various Indian tribes and waged a particularly fierce battle at Panatacat (now Escuintla, in Guatemala). Crossing the River Paxaco he reached for the first time the lands of the powerful Kingdom of Cuzcatlán, about June 18, 1524. After encounters with the Indians, who fled to the mountains from where they continually harassed the Spaniards, it is said that Alvarado fought against them and the so-called great chiefs, Atlacatl and Atonal, whom historians have held up to admiration. Actually, they are a myth, as the names of the chiefs of the Cuzcatlán Indians who fought against Alvarado have not been handed down in history.[1]

Alvarado waged a fierce battle in Acaxutla where he was wounded in one leg, and was lame for the rest of his life. He was obliged to return to Guatemala. During the whole period, Alvarado was six months and fifteen days absent from his headquarters in that country.

The first mass was celebrated by the army's chaplain, Juan Godínez, on August 6. It was a great disappointment to Alvarado that he could not spend the winter in the warm climate of Cuzcatlán.

In synthesis, from then on history gives the following facts: once back in Guatemala, Alvarado quickly put his affairs in order before leaving for Hibueras (now Honduras), where he expected to meet Cortés, having left his brother Jorge de Alvarado in charge of his Cuzcatlán conquest.

The Indian chiefs rebelled and joined the Chaparrestique, Guaymangos, Izalco, and other nearby Indian tribes, rapidly swelling the ranks to form a formidable army against the Spaniards. In the meantime Alvarado, arriving in Hibueras, found that Cortés had sailed for Mexico, so he immediately started his return journey. He brought with him Luis Marín and Bernal Díaz del Castillo, the famous soldier-historian of colonial days. The Indians from Oceloclán (Usulután), on hearing that white men had arrived on the opposite bank of the Lempa River, gathered to prevent Alvarado's crossing

---

1 According to: *II Carta de Relación de Alvarado á Cortés. Julio 1524.*

over. Nevertheless he managed to drive the Indians back to a high hill (Peñol) and forded this turbulent stream.

However, Alvarado and his army were not the only white men to set foot in this territory. In 1522, Gil Gonzáles Dávila led an expedition coming up from the south, together with Andrés Niño, the discoverer of the Bay of Fonseca. That unpleasant man, Pedro Arias de Avila, best known as Pedrarias Dávila, had conquered and cruelly treated the Indians in the southern part of the Isthmus. Toward the end of 1529, he sent Martín Estete to conquer the regions now known as El Salvador, where the former Spanish invaders had not been able to advance. Estete took with him ninety horsemen and one-hundred ten infantrymen, and entered this country from the south by the region of the Kingdom of Chaparrestique, now San Miguel. He was the cruelest of all the cruel *conquistadores*.

To return to Alvarado and his handful of soldiers, confronted by the Indians, they had great difficulties in fording the River Lempa, which the heavy rains had swollen. According to a narrative of one of the soldiers: "so we cut a huge tree called *Ceiba* and therefrom made a canoe, no greater one had ever been seen in these parts, and it took us five days to cross the river, having great scarcity of corn. When we crossed the river, we found villages belonging to the Chaparrestique Indians . . . where our soldiers found food. . . . The Indians had retired to El Peñol." Some of the Spanish soldiers had come to look for Alvarado and his men so as to help them. They met in a place called Choluteca. Later the captains of Pedrarias attempted to divide the conquest with Pedro Alvarado, but nothing resulted from this conference, and Alvarado proceeded towards the province of Cuzcatlán and thence to Guatemala and later to Spain.

Captain Diego de Rojas, who led the small army that had come to help Alvarado at the Lempa River, heard about the Spaniards who had come up from the south. Rojas naturally imagined Martín de Estete to be friendly and prepared to join him—a great mistake, which he soon found out to his sorrow, as Estete did not hesitate to take him prisoner.

Estete had committed atrocities against the Indians of the region of San Miguel, which so angered the Chaparrestique chiefs that they gathered their clans and descended from their strongholds eager to march and fight against this new army of white men. The soldiers, when informed of the facts, turned on their heels and immediately sent word to Guatemala as to what was happening. The authorities in Guatemala were indignant at Pedrarias' temerity in presuming to encroach on territory that was rightfully the conquest of Alvarado and his army. Captain Francisco López, at the head of a small contingent, was sent from Guatemala to detain the advancing Spaniards coming from the south.

Estete, finding himself at a loss, retired to a site where he imagined he could establish a permanent capital of the country, as his chief Pedrarias wished him to take possession of a place in the name of the King—or rather for his own aggrandizement. He advanced to Perulápan, giving that place the grandiose name of "Ciudad de los Caballeros," and demanding that he should be named Captain and Governor General of San Salvador, offering as a bait the inducement that in future neither he nor any of his Spanish followers would take Indian slaves.

His satisfaction was short-lived, as neither the Spaniards nor the Indians accepted his promises, and he was obliged to take the remnants of his army and again flee south, not stopping until he reached the other side of the Lempa River, where Estete quietly abandoned his people to their fate and vanished. His army, without a leader, was at a loss. Part of the men disbanded and went south; others made peace with the Spaniards who had pursued them, and returned to Guatemala.

Pedro de Alvarado, who had just returned from his trip to Spain, and was in Mexico, on hearing what had happened to his newly acquired conquests because of Martín Estete's invasion of the provinces of Chaparrestique and Cuzcatlán, hurried to Guatemala where he arrived in 1530, to learn that Estete had been obliged to abandon his boasted conquests. So Alvarado sent Captain Luis Moscoso to pacify the turbulent country, completely disorganized through Indian revolts, Spanish misadventures, and in general in a chaotic state. Captain Luis Moscoso managed to establish a town, now known as San Miguel, on the banks of the River Lempa.

The task of pacifying the Indians continued after the country was cleared of enemies. However, it was not easy, as the Indians of this territory were not at all amenable to peaceful overtures, and it was not until 1537 that those in the region of Chaparrestique were finally subdued. As late as 1539, the Indians, despite many set-backs, again arose and tried to overthrow the colonial regime, but without success.

IV

SAN SALVADOR

State and City

PEDRO DE ALVARADO was not successful in establishing a Spanish town; but by orders of his brother Diego de Alvarado a Spanish city was established; in the precise information in the *Libro de Actas del Ayuntamiento de Guatemala, 1524-1530*, it is stated that in 1525 a Spanish village was created, having a *cabildo* which, on May 6, 1525, named as its first mayor *(alcalde)* a man by the name of Diego de Holguín. It also stated that Gonzalo de Alvarado established in April, 1525, the Villa de San Salvador.

So many sites have been mentioned as the various capitals of El Salvador that it is a question as to which was first. However, documents give this site more or less accurately near the territory of the Cuzcatlán Indians, in a valley called La Bermuda (very probably so named by one of the first Spaniards to settle there, by the name of Bermudez). The Cuzcatlán Indians did not take kindly to their new neighbors. This first village was abandoned and provisionally re-established on a site called Los Almendros, near what is now Suchitoto.

It is also definitely known that after the Spaniards had pacified the Indians of La Costa del Bálsamo and the restless Cuzcatlán people, the town was moved in 1528 by order of Captain Jorge de Alvarado; In 1545 it was moved to El Valle de las Hamacas, (Valley of the Hammocks, or Cuzcatlán), and in 1546 was given the title city. Though the city was actually moved, it is more than likely that some of the Spaniards remained on the former site, La Bermuda, later known as the Aldea o Villa de la Bermuda, which completely disappeared in a deluge of rain in 1541. (A legend currently

24

believed states that the site of La Bermuda attracts electrical
storms.) This is probably due to the afore-mentioned storm
in 1541. It is more probable that it was abandoned because
the heavy rains washed away the best soil and thereby agriculture failed.

The name San Salvador given to the first establishment is
variously interpreted: it was derived from its patron saint
under whose protection the city was placed, El Salvador del
Mundo, or Santísimo Salvador. The fact that on August 6,
the day dedicated to that saint, a decisive battle was won
against the Cuzcatlán Indians may have had some influence
on the choice of the name. On the other hand, the first
alcalde, Diego de Holguín, had been a very prominent member of the community of San Salvador de Bayamo in Spain
and may have decided to perpetuate this name in his new
jurisdiction, later extended to the province.

The town was moved hither and yonder for many years,
like a traveler packing his belongings into his old kit bag
and departing for lands less troublesome. It never was stable,
and the various moves are hopelessly mixed up.

Earthquakes were a constant menace, as well as Indian up-
risings, but in the end the inhabitants always returned to the
Valley of the Hammocks, so aptly named for its constantly
shaking earth. A definite move seems to have been made in
1545, after a very heavy earthquake, and the town was established on its original site in another angle of the Valley
of Quezaltepeque, but it was later transferred to its present
site.

The name Cuzcatlán is derived from the Indian, meaning
"Land of precious things." The Indian name of this valley is
Quetzalcoatitán, meaning "Place of the plumed serpent,"
but the Spaniards called it Valle de las Hamacas, and the
town, Villa de San Salvador.

The first priest of the village was Padre Pedro Jiménez.
The town prospered, and in 1546, His Gracious Majesty the
Emperor Charles V conceded to it the title Ciudad.

The year 1575 started badly with heavy and continued
earthquakes. San Salvador was especially affected, and the

King, hearing of the damage, ordered the religious orders in Guatemala to send members of their communities to aid the people. This date is often taken mistakenly as the beginning of the permanent city of San Salvador, if you can call "permanent" a place that has been destroyed so repeatedly.

In that year the city had five-hundred Spanish inhabitants. Some years previously the Auditor of the Audiencia de los Confines expressed great surprise (when he passed through this town on his way home from Gracias a Dios to Guatemala) that, despite all the upheavals the place had gone through, the city had prospered and good buildings had been erected. It was due to their good construction that the heavy earthquakes did not ruin all of them. However, in 1581 and 1594 much damage was done; an eruption completely destroyed the city, and the terror-stricken inhabitants fled to neighboring villages. Heavy damage was also caused by the earthquakes of 1659 and 1798, which were really catastrophic. The inhabitants had little opportunity to forge ahead materially or to develop culture, as constant seeking for safety seems to have been their lot.

For many years the city was literally constructed of cardboard, with thatched roofs on the houses. The heroic inhabitants nevertheless persisted, and finally achieved a capital city worthy of their efforts.

COLONIAL LIFE

Colonial life in the Salvador area was much like that of the other provinces of the kingdom of Guatemala. Administratively, it was divided into two independent provinces under the rule of the Capitanía General of Guatemala: the province of San Salvador, and the province of Sonsonate, though figuratively dependent on the authorities in Guatemala, who sent their officials to San Salvador, were practically independent of their superior officers, and did pretty much as they pleased, as long as they conformed to some semblance of the rules and regulations sent out by Spain. The province of San Salvador was one of the four *Intendencias* of the *Capitanía General,* comprising four districts: San Salvador, Santa Ana, San Vicente, and San Miguel. The province of San Salvador or Cuzcatlán was the most important and most populated. It was governed by an *Intendente,* who resided in the district of San Salvador with delegates in the other districts. Each *Intendente* had an *Asesor* (Counsellor) and a *Tesorero* Real (Royal Treasurer).

The Ecclesiastical authorities were ordered by His Majesty King Charles V, in a *Cédula Real* (1574), to proceed immediately to build convents wherever it was necessary, and therefore the President, Pedro de Vilalobos, ordered that churches and convents should be erected in Cuzcatlán and in the province of Sonsonate (Izalco).

Socially San Salvador was isolated, for communication with the other capitals of the provinces and that of the Kingdom was not easy. Hence the people took matters into their own hands, and disported themselves at their pleasure, probably more so and in a much gayer atmosphere than even in the capital in Guatemala. People who live on the brink of danger, where every minute may be the end of their existence, make the most of their time and enjoy themselves to the full. Their styles and their way of living were those that they had brought from Spain.

Mail took months to reach the colonies. It was taken care of by the *Estafetas Postales* (postal offices) along the route from North to South to Porto Bello, and thence with mails from South America to Europe.

All the Alvarado brothers prodded the Spanish, especially Pedro, who kept nagging them to help him to get ready his expeditions to Peru, where he went to help Almagro and Pizarro and ended up in the most unfortunate adventure of his life. He was forced to barter his equipment in exchange for some money and in 1535 departed to his conquests in Central America. The Spaniards in the city of San Salvador, despite their oath of allegiance to stay and settle permanently in the city, protested energetically against this treatment, and many departed for lands to the south.

As with all the Spanish conquests, this one was marked by the extermination of the Indians whom the Spaniards either dispersed in the woods or congregated around the religious centers. During the first years of the conquest, Spain prohibited young girls from going to the colonies, except by royal permission, and consequently the intermingling of the two races was rapid. This may account for the small Indian population of today in this country. However, it was also prohibited by royal decree (1551) that bachelors should come to the colonies.

The country rapidly assumed a different aspect. The Spaniards brought seeds and plants from their homeland. Great quantities of sugarcane and other important crops were planted. Indigo, a plant of America, was intensively cultivated and the dye material used extensively.

It did not take long for the Spaniards to adapt themselves either from necessity or liking, to the food that they found. Very soon corn, black beans, peppers, and other indigeneous foods of the Americas were incorporated in their diet. The lack of doctors naturally turned them toward the Indian methods of healing, and so the medicinal herbs and potions were adopted in the colonial pharmacopœia.

Commerce was most active. In fact, San Salvador was the crossroads not alone for historical invasions from the north and south, but as a trading center, and thus became the theater of all historical happenings of the Isthmus. Through this country came large pack mule trains flanked by human *cargadores* (cargo bearers) bearing quinine from the forests of Honduras, its own indigo, gold and silver from wherever it could be acquired, and treasures stolen from the conquered Indians. The Quinto Real (Royal Fifth) was one of the rich cargoes that went through this territory on its way to Porto Bello, to be transferred to galleons sailing overseas. It was fortunate if such cargoes reached their destinations, for piratical depredations were frequent during the sixteenth and seventeenth centuries.

A contributing factor to a rather disturbed life led by the inhabitants was that the Indians in this part of Central

America never quite submitted to the rule of the Spaniards. On the other hand, discontent with the local governors who were sent out to administer affairs was also the cause of continual unrest, and San Salvador was constantly in turmoil over Spanish customs barriers, terrestrial calamities, Indian troubles, and unpleasant local governors, all of which made life untenable. It is not strange, therefore, that this place was the cradle of the most influential move toward the independence of Central American countries.

Nevertheless, some parts of the country were not enthusiastic about casting in their lot with the conspirators, and refused to enter into the plot, which continued to simmer for years. The young descendants of the Spaniards—*criollos*— and the *mestizos* who had received good educations, however, refused to remain under the rule of the *chapetones* (those individuals born in Spain), and revolted against machinations of the officials in Guatemala and those governing the provinces, so they were eager to help in any movement that might change a situation that could not be worse. They did not care what the change might imply—all they desired was a change. They had observed the way of living in Guatemala city during their school years there, and on their return could not adjust themselves quietly to the environment of a more backward and continually unsettled country, such as the state of San Salvador during the close of the colonial era.

They met secretly here and there, efficiently aided by some members of the clergy who also desired a change because of the tardiness of instructions and aid from their orders, and the general chaos in one and all of these orders.

The last years of colonial rule were strenuous indeed. The restrictions Spain put on exports from America, the general state of poverty throughout all the provinces, failures of crops, epidemics, and a general feeling of disquiet helped further to fan the general feeling of unrest.

INDEPENDENCE

V

THE STRUGGLE FOR INDEPENDENCE

IN 1811, the Governor General of the Kingdom of Guatemala was Captain General José Bustamente y Guerra, and a priest, José Matías Delgado, who had been educated at the University of San Carlos Borromeo in Guatemala, was in charge of the church of La Merced in San Salvador. Together with Manuel José Arce, Nicolás Manuel Vicente Aguilar, and Juan Manuel Rodríguez they met and conspired to seize the ammunition in the city. On November 5, 1811, Padre Delgado arose to launch from the towers of his church the first cry for independence from Spain that was heard in all Central America.

When the news reached Guatemala, Colonel José Aycinena went to San Salvador to squelch any further movement in that direction. Thus, for the time being, a simulated peace was restored, at least superficially. The conspiracy in Guatemala that aimed toward liberation from Spain failed in 1813. Meanwhile Captain General Bustamante was succeeded in 1818 by Captain General Carlos Unrutia Montoya, a very tolerant leader and ruler who closed his eyes and ears to the underground work of the people, both in Guatemala and in San Salvador, where the flame of independence was spreading.

Later Brigadier Gabino Gainza was named Captain General. He also did nothing to hinder the plans for independence. In San Salvador active campaigning succeeded in arousing most of the country against Spain, this despite the fact that several regions of the country had declared their refusal to take part in the early attempts at independence. Naturally this attitude pleased the mother country, and the Regency in Spain awarded a prize for their loyalty. Furthermore, San Miguel was granted the title, *La Muy Noble y Muy Leal Ciudad de San Miguel*. San Vicente was granted the title Ciudad, and Santa Ana was raised to the status of Villa de Santa Ana (the titles *Ciudad* and *Villa* must not be taken in the literal sense and translated into town and village, but were words of honor and distinction, steps toward acquiring higher and more distinguished titles). These three places remained loyal, and again in the year 1814, when another proclamation for independence was made, they sent troops to help squelch the movement.

The general unrest, discontent, and resentment against Spain could not be quenched, and it filtered insidiously throughout the country so that these last three strongholds of monarchical sentiments were affected; in 1821 the whole country was united during the eventful happenings that took place in Guatemala.

It seemed as though daily either His Royal Majesty in Spain or the *Real Audiencia* of New Spain announced a new decree, and new *Cédulas* containing prohibitions and more prohibitions were decreed for the colonies. One of them (in 1580) prohibited the transportation of merchandise overland through Central America in the Kingdom of Guatemala, because, since the *Derecho de Almojarifazgo* (maritime tax) had been decreed, maritime commerce had perceptibly declined.

Another decree (1565) advised the colonies that only foreigners with permission issued by His Royal Majesty the King might reside in these countries. This edict was later canceled, but it was stated that foreigners residing in these countries must contribute their share of taxes for the maintenance of the Windward Fleet *(Flota de Barlovento)*.

As the years went by and matters grew worse, as each decree complicated the commerce and other activities of the colonies to the point where activity declined or was completely at a standstill, it is not surprising that once the movement for independence had started, it gathered momentum like a rolling stone.

The Royalists in Guatemala were suspicious of Brigadier Gaínza, and it later transpired that their suspicions were well founded. Gaínza was anxious to maintain his own position, but blind to any meetings and movements which tended toward separation from Spain. The Royalist party was sadly depleted and only the *Oficiales Reales,* the Church authorities, and a handful of others who had their own interests to further by remaining in the Party continued as loyal subjects to Spain. Added to this was the problem of the hordes of Indians who had to be kept in bondage. Despite the intense jealousy of one province for the other, all were united in a common hatred of Spain during those last years of colonial life. In truth, it could hardly be called life, for it was a bare existence for the wretched inhabitants of the kingdom, and the farther away they were from the capital, the less interest was taken in their welfare. By this time a change—any change—was welcome to end the drabness of their existence.

A memorable meeting was called for September 15, 1821, in the City of La Nueva Guatemala de la Asunción, for the purpose of considering a momentous document that had arrived from Mexico. The Captain General, Gabino Gaínza, most of the representatives of the other provinces, who had been fortunate enough to arrive on time, and crowds of other people were present at this meeting: Royalists, the Archbishop, members of the clergy, and all the leading men. In the village of Iguala in Mexico, Emperor Agustín Iturbide, backed by the Royalist party, formulated the document that was laid before the assembly. This later became known as the *Plan de Iguala,* or *El Plan de las Tres Garantias.* It provided (1) that Mexico and the Kingdom of Guatemala should invite a Prince of Spain, preferably Fernando VII, to come to the New World and rule them jointly as an independent empire; (2) that the Catholic Church should be the supreme and only religious authority; and (3) that the *chapetones* (those born in Spain) and the creoles should bury the hatchet and live in peace and harmony forever.

Brigadier Gaínza moved that the *Plan de Iguala* be adopted. A tremendous uproar greeted his suggestion, because the majority had but one idea in mind, and that was complete independence from Spain and every other power. The Royalists withdrew from the meeting, realizing that the situation was very unfavorable to their side. The Salvadoreans, headed by José Matías Delgado, were most emphatic in their refusal to join in the *Plan de Iguala*. They declared that only complete independence from Spain and from every other country would satisfy them. Doctor Delgado was one of the signers of the famous Act whereby independence from Spain was declared on that same day.

Emperor Agustín Iturbide, when the news reached him of all that was transpiring in the south, was in no mood to have his plan upset. He succeeded in persuading the provinces to join him, with the exception of San Salvador. He sent General Vicente Filísola with troops to bring the Salvadoreans to his side. In the meantime, battles were being fought against Guatemalan troops. The Salvadoreans under Manuel José Arce were victorious in the first encounters, but when Filísola arrived fortunes changed, and the Mexican general made short work of his opponents. Nevertheless, news reached the Mexican general that Iturbide's empire had come to a sudden end, and he turned on his heel and fled for home.

With the Mexican Empire ended and the rest of the provinces freed, they joined San Salvador, and with the exception of Chiapas, north of Guatemala, united to form in 1823 the *República Federal de Centro América,* also known as *Las Provincias Unidas de Centro América.* General Manuel José Arce was elected first President of the federation. He did not last long in this post, and the Liberal Party, which opposed the Church, as against the Conservatives who supported it, were active in San Salvador, Honduras, and Guatemala. Under the leadership of General Francisco Morazán, a Hondurean, the Liberals overthrew President Arce and elected Morazán as President. (The

Liberals were in favor of the federal system. The *Garcistas* or aristocrats wanted a unitarian system.)

Each state of the Union had its own Chief of State, and the General Assembly of San Salvador, composed of forty-one representatives, on June 24, 1823, elected Juan Manuel Rodríguez as the chief of this state. A movement to make independent states of the departments of Santa Ana and Sonsonate failed, for the Federal Congress dissolved it as its inception, in the same way it had ended the already established state of Los Altos in Guatemala.

The National Constituent Assembly on June 29, 1823, presided over by Padre Delgado, decreed that "The Provinces of Central America are free and independent of Spain, of Mexico, and of any other power of the Old as well as of the New World, and must not be the property or inheritance of any family or person."

The First General Congress convened in 1823-1824, adopted a constitution, and voted for the federal system of government. Padre Delgado was the first to sign the *Carta Constitutiva*. To the glory of this country and of this Assembly, a decree was signed whereby slaves were to be liberated for all time in these countries. An ancient Salvadorean priest, Dr. José Simeón Cañas, with tears streaming down his face, made this famous pronouncement: "I drag myself to this place, and even if I were dying, dying I would come to make a statement for the benefit of suffering humanity. I implore the meeting today to declare that our brothers, the slaves, should be freed. . . ." The decree was unanimously approved with a great show of enthusiasm. Immediately and first of all slave holders, the members of this Assembly freed their own slaves.

The federation of the former provinces of the Kingdom of Guatemala was beset by repeated wars and disturbances, thus depriving it of freedom to organize and become established on a firm footing, both politically and ecclesiastically. Nevertheless, in 1838 the Central American Congress granted the states liberty to organize themselves as they wished, while preserving a popular and representative form of government.[1] On February 18, 1841, the State of San Salvador adopted its constitution, under which the people became free and independent with the right to govern themselves in the manner best suited to them. This country assumed the title *La República de El Salvador* on January 25, 1849. However, from 1841 it was absolutely autonomous, having in that year adopted the constitution decreed by the famous Constituent Assembly of 1824.

The province of San Salvador during the colonial period was governed by the laws of Spain, and the *Real Audiencia* (Superior Court of Justice) in Guatemala decided all judicial matters. Don Juan Manuel Rodríguez, the first Chief of State of this country, organized in 1824 the Salvadorean Judicial Power. The Constitution of 1841 decreed that this power was vested in the Supreme Court of Justice *(La Corte Suprema de Justicia)*, and several lower courts. In 1886 the Constitution was changed, providing that the judicial power must be exercised by the Supreme Court of Justice and its lower courts *(Cámeras de Segunda y Tercera Instancia)*. Criminal matters must be tried by jury; at the same time the rights of appeal and habeas corpus were decreed.

[1] As a matter of interest, the San Salvador National Congress was the first to decree (on May 30, 1838) the liberty of self-determination.

VI

EVOLUTION AND REVOLUTION

FROM the time independence was declared from Spain, the history of El Salvador is but a succession of revolts and wars. When not busy sending an army to combat their neighbor, Guatemala, the Salvadoreans were engaged in defending their country against the threats of invasion from their other neighbors, Honduras and Nicaragua.

In 1826 wars broke out between Guatemala and El Salvador, because the Guatemalan *émigrés,* who had been given a safe asylum in El Salvador, started fomenting trouble. General Manuel José Arce,[1] the President of Guatemala, at the head of a large army invaded El Salvador, because it would not acknowledge his leadership. After several battles in which General Arce was victorious, El Salvador asked for peace. It was not conceded until after General Arce had occupied the region of Santa Ana several times and caused tremendous unrest in all the country.

Before going any further, a word must be said about General Francisco Morazán, who, though born in Honduras, was most active in taking part in all the revolts in the other countries of Central America, as well as in taking part in their internal politics. He was the outstanding figure in favor of the Union of Central America and has been variously appraised by historians, according to their country of origin. Nevertheless his name crops up repeatedly, and in El Salvador it was to be reckoned with.

In 1828 Guatemala and El Salvador were at war until peace was signed at La Ceiba. However, continual trouble

---

[1] General Arce was elected the first President of the Federation of Central America. He was a Salvadorean by birth.

kept brewing because El Salvador consistently showed
friendship for the newly formed Estado de los Altos, which
aroused the antagonism of President Carrera in Guatemala.

General Morazán arrived in Salvador as a refugee from
Honduras at the beginning of 1827. From then on there was
not a battle in which he did not take some part, always with
the idea of a future united Central America. In one battle
where Honduras was united with Nicaragua against El Salvador, he, together with General Trinidad Cabañas was victorious against his opponents who had occupied a strategic
position on a hill, El Gualcho. General Ferrera, in 1839,
brought his Honduran army against El Salvador, but the
people of Honduras were not in accord and several regions
of that country—Curarén, Santa Rosa, Texiguat, and Goascorán—asked for annexation to Salvador.

With an army led by Morazán and called *Ejército Aliado
Protecor de la Ley* (Allied Army Protector of the Law), the
Salvadoreans again prepared for a war with Guatemala, and
returned triumphant to their country. Battles and counter-
battles, revolutions and internal trouble were the fate of this
country in the following years. Morazán was named president in 1832 and again in 1839, but he had all Central
America against him during his tenancy in office, and more
than once he had to fight the Hondurean and Nicaraguan
armies. One outstanding occasion must be mentioned when
General Bernardo Méndez, united with the Nicaraguans,
took San Miguel and started into the interior of this country. A decisive battle was fought near the estate of Espíritu
Santo against the combined forces of Méndez and Francisco
Ferrera. In this battle, though he was victorious, Morazán
was wounded. The victorious Salvadoreans also triumphed
in the battle of Perulapán, and in 1840 marched against
Guatemala. In this encounter Morazán was not so lucky and
had to return to Salvador, and together with a group of his
generals left the country. This was the direct cause of the
dissolution of the Federation.

Later Morazán appeared on the island of Martín Pérez
(in the Gulf of Fonseca) and called for volunteers to attempt

once more the union of Central America. Bad luck pursued him and he was killed in Costa Rica (September 15, 1842), having expressed a wish that he might be buried in El Salvador. It was not until later that his remains were brought there and deposited in Sonsonate. Later they were moved to Santa Ana and finally interred in San Salvador.

During all these years of turmoil, a great figure in the history of the country was Gerardo Barrios Espinosa (1813-1865). As a youth he was fired with enthusiasm by the fame of Morazán, ranging himself on his side, and throughout his life was an enthusiastic upholder of the union of Central America. Barrios commanded a division in the battle of El Gualcho and was with Morazán when he entered Guatemala, at which time he was promoted to Captain. He took part in the battle of San Pedro Perulapán, and because he led the assault on the bell tower of the church where General Ferrera had fortified himself, Barrios was promoted to Lieutenant Colonel.

General Francisco Malespín was President in 1844 when another revolt started, and war was declared between Guatemala and El Salvador. The army, consisting mostly of *Coquimbos (Morazanistas* or *unionists)*, had Colonel Barrios in command of the second division. General Malespín personally led this army to occupy the town of Jutiapa in Guatemala. The Coquimbos, impatient at the slow progress, plotted against Malespín who, on discovering the plot, signed a peace pact with Guatemala, dissolved the army, and returned to El Salvador to reassume the presidency. As General Malespín felt he had been badly treated when a soldier with Morazán, he sided with Carrera in Guatemala and became as strong an antiunionist as Carrera himself.

General Trinidad Cabañas had gathered many sympathizers and revolted against Malespín, convinced that the latter was not doing what he could against the Guatemalans. When the refugees from this revolt migrated to Nicaragua, that country refused to give them up, and Malespín, authorized by the Assembly, declared war on Nicaragua and Honduras. Furthermore, the Unionist Party was now quite convinced that as long as President Carrera and Malespín were hand in glove, no union was possible. As a last resort, Malespín united with Bishop Viteri, but nothing was achieved, and on November 25, 1846, General Malespín was assassinated. His head was cut off and brought from San Salvador on the point of a lance to a place on the road to Mejicanos and exhibited to the populace. The place is still known as *La Calavera* (the skull) because of this episode.

General Gerardo Barrios was elected President of El Salvador in 1858 and re-elected in 1860. Heavy seismic disturbances occurred and destroyed the capital, which he ordered moved to Cojutepeque. Four years later he again transferred it to its former site. Barrios was brave and though outwardly a peaceful and kind man, he never could resist a good fight. In 1857 he took his army to Nicaragua to oppose an invasion by an American named William Walker, who with his followers had the wild idea of conquering Central America. Barrios also fought in 1863 the invading army of Guatemala, driving the Guatemalans out of El Salvador. He marched triumphantly to Cojutepeque, where he was acclaimed General in Chief of the army and eight days of festivities were declared when he entered the city of San Salvador.

During the years of his administration, great evolution took place in the country. He helped to revive agriculture, which had fallen lamentably into neglect during the later colonial period and early republican regime. He ordered young coffee trees from Brazil to replace those that had become useless. In 1860, under his administration, the first *Código Civil* was decreed. He transferred the capital back to the old site, and also transferred the body of his idol, Morazán. He was a great factor in furthering education, was much interested in a better school system, and was the founder of the Normal School and the Academy of Music and Arts. Doctor Lorenzo Montúfar [1] was invited to come from Guatemala to San Miguel and establish a well-organized institu-

[1] Dr. Montúfar was a great man in the history of his time, in all branches of learning.

tion of learning in that city, which would be the pioneer and example for other scholastic centers.

General Gerardo Barrios traveled extensively through Spain, France, and Great Britain, and in Madrid he formed a lasting friendship with Louis Napoleon Bonaparte; visiting Rome, he was granted an audience by Pope Pius IX. In 1864 General Barrios was exiled and took refuge in Costa Rica. The rest of the Central American Republics severed diplomatic relations with that country because she refused to expel Barrios. It is a lasting blot on the escutcheon of El Salvador that, after he returned in 1865 to El Salvador, despite every attempt to save his life, he was shot on August 29 of that year at the foot of the Ceiba tree in the cemetery of San Salvador. Nevertheless, later-day historians give him credit for being a true patriot and brave man.

Returning to the early years of independence, the well-known priest, Dr. Matías Delgado, had worked hard so that San Salvador might be granted the honor of episcopal rank. This was accomplished in 1822. It caused untold turmoil when Dr. Delgado was named the first Bishop and the Cathedral the head of the Bishopric of San Salvador. The Congress heard Dr. Delgado's oath of office, and the Assembly in a body and all the authorities heard the Te Deum in the newly named Cathedral. The Guatemalan ecclesiastical authorities did not approve of El Salvador's being converted into a Bishopric, and trouble issued. The Archbishop in Guatemala in 1824 declared null and void the nomination of Delgado as Bishop and in July, 1825, both sides took their troubles to Rome for a hearing before Pope Leo XII. In 1826, everything that had taken place in San Salvador was declared illigitimate and contrary to the decision of the Holy See, and Dr. Delgado, as a simple *vicario,* continued in the ecclesiastical government of his people in the province of San Salvador. So ended this tempest in a teapot.

In 1842 the question of nominating a Bishop for El Salvador was again agitated. Nominally the first Bishop, Jorge Viteri y Ungo, was consecrated in Rome on December 29, and all the formalities were gone through. During his tenacy in office he consecrated in San Salvador at the Cathedral the new Archbishop of Guatemala, Francisco García de Peláez. His Holiness the Pope had been much taken with the new Bishop and had expressed himself as follows: "Tell your people at El Salvador that I do not send them a Bishop, but rather a Pope, because you are endowed with powers which are almost similar to mine."

Among his committee, when he arrived in El Salvador, were three friars who were later ordained in the new Cathedral of the city. One was not a real priest, although this fact was not discovered until he became the priest of Zacatecoluca. It is told that this priest, celebrating a mass on Easter Sunday, ended by singing: "Alleluia, Alleluia, cada uno con la suya," and continued, "con su obligación." ("Alleluia, Alleluia, everyone do as he chooses . . . I mean, with their duties.") The priest got himself disliked and suddenly disappeared from the scene.

Another of these priests, a Colombian, was immediately nicknamed "Fray Venemo" (Poison Friar) because of his virulent sermons and eloquent oratory. Bishop Viteri was a fanatic and soon converted his people to fanaticism with no intellectual foundation. His sermons incited the populace against infidels and those who called themselves liberals, and he was not above mixing in political events, thus getting himself hopelessly involved on all sides.

A historical event during these years of evolution and revolutions was the uprising in 1833 of the Indians at whose head was Anastasio Aquino, a native of Santiago Nonualco, who with his hordes committed depredations in the smaller villages near his home. Gathering strength with thousands of Indians in a war against the whites, he endeavored to force his way by sundry battles into the town of San Vicente (see page 196), and he set fire to the outskirts. Don Manuel Mariano Azmitia, much respected by the lower classes, heroically went out to interview the Indian chief, and was able to restrain the Indians for a while from further violence by offering a banquet to Aquino. Aquino, after feeding well at his host's table, called his retinue and sacked the town, taking possession of all the silver and gold plate, cutlery, and other things belonging to his host.

At the church of la Ermita de Nuestra Señora del Pilar, he entered the chapel of San José and, with a grandiose gesture, snatched the great crown of gold and emeralds from the sacred image. Placing the crown on his head he proclaimed himself King Anastasio Aquino and was carried on the shoulders of his mob through the city. Aquino took as hostages many of the ladies of the town. An Indian lieutenant intervened in Aquino's amorous intentions toward one of the ladies, Matilde Marín, a beautiful girl from San Vicente. Though he treated her in a courteous manner, refusing to let any of his Indians mistreat her even by looks or words, she was hopelessly despondent, for Aquino intended to wed her after killing María, his wife.

As soon as the government authorities in San Salvador under the Chief of State, Mariano Prado, heard of these events, they immediately sent troops against the Indians. The frustrated lieutenant had turned traitor and informer, contacted the troops, and showed them the way to the place where Aquino and his hordes were encamped. Aquino fled to the mountains, but he was caught and hung in April, 1833. Matilde Marín managed to escape in the encounter with the government troops.

To make matters more lively, outside powers began to trouble the Central American states during the Federation and after it. One of the causes of trouble was the debt incurred by Central America to Great Britain, which later, after the Federation was ended, was divided among the different states, or rather the new nations. The Government of El Salvador declared at the outset that its share was onerous and the whole business had been unjustly managed. The British Consul, Frederick Chatwick, with a British man-of-war occupied the island of El Tigre (in the Bay of Fonseca), and harassed El Salvador. At the beginning of 1850, British gunboats blocked the ports of La Unión and Acajutla. Finally matters were arranged through the good offices of the United States of America.

Another great unionist was President Justo Rufino Barrios of Guatemala, but El Salvador and Guatemala were again aroused against each other when a new Union was attempted. In the battle of Chalchuapa President Barrios of Guatemala met his death, and thus ended another war between these countries (1885).

Nevertheless, during all these years of turmoil many reforms were carried out in El Salvador. Buildings were erected in the capital city and education was given a forward impulse. So the years of turmoil came to an end and El Salvador entered into the modern period, which might be called its greatest.

VII

THE UNION OF CENTRAL AMERICA

FROM the time when the five states of Central America formed the ephemeral *Provincias Unidas del Centro de América,* which brought no lasting benefit to any of them, these countries have attempted a total or partial union at various times. Most of them have lasted but a short time. The first Union lasted until 1840, and despite the best intentions, amity and understanding did not thrive; in fact, the petty jealousies, political intrigues, and the general state of depression in all the states made a heterogeneous union an impossibility. The Indian and the Spanish backgrounds of the five countries were so different that it is understandable that they could not amalgamate into one great country. At the time this is written (1956) much is being done to further a better understanding among the Central American countries.[1]

In 1842, Nicaragua, Honduras, and Salvador combined to form a provisional government in Chinandega. Although it did not prosper, it was attempted again in 1844. All Central America united in 1854-56, with a sacred fire burning in every heart, a union of spirits, but it was ineffective since most of the countries were governed by the politically conservative party, very much set against a union. However, a union was urgently needed for a combined effort against William Walker and his filibusters, who had invaded Nicaragua with the intention of extending their conquest to the rest of Central America.

In 1876, a plenipotentiary council signed a pact whereby

[1] The O.D.E.C.A. (Organization of the Central American States) is a symbol of the future union of Central American countries.

a union was to be formed, but instead, Guatemala, Honduras, and El Salvador disagreed, and this attempt at unity ended in war.

Francisco Morazán was perhaps the outstanding figure who worked for a union of Central America. This Hondurean General invaded several of the countries to force a union, but was unsuccessful, though his ideas were the inspiration for more than one of the leaders in the different countries of Central America.

President Justo Rufino Barrios of Guatemala was a great worker in the cause of union. In 1855 he proclaimed a union, declaring himself the Supreme Military Chief. President Rafael Zaldívar of El Salvador and the presidents of Costa Rica and Nicaragua energetically protested against this, and sent an appeal to President Porfirio Díaz in Mexico. General Justo Rufino Barrios was advised that the Congress in each of the above-named countries had emphatically decreed against his military government, to which he replied: that he "would carry it out, nevertheless, and by force if necessary." He was succeeded in Guatemala by President Lisandro Barillas, who was not at all enthusiastic about a union, so the scheme for a time was in abeyance.

In 1889 El Salvador sent out invitations to the other countries to send plenipotentiaries to convene and discuss a union. Nothing came of it, as a military uprising in El Salvador, which ended with the death of President Francisco Menéndez, stopped the parley. In 1895, Doctor Policarpo Bonilla, President of Honduras, invited the countries to Amapala for a conference. El Salvador and Nicaragua were the only ones represented, and they signed with Honduras *El Pacto de Unión,* which decreed the "Greater Republic of Central America" (*La República Mayor de Centro América*). The Republic lasted a scant two years.

Nicaragua in 1898 again attempted to call a meeting which decreed *La Constitución de los Estados Unidos de Centro América* with a provisional counsel, granting powers to the executives to call for elections, whereby a president and federal congress might be chosen. This meeting opened with much enthusiasm in Amapala on November 1 of that year, but after thirteen days a military uprising in El Salvador put an end to the dream of a Federation.

Doctor Francisco Beltrán, the President of Honduras, once more in 1917 tried his hand at forming a union, and asked the plenipotentiaries to meet in Guatemala. Severe earthquakes in that year destroyed that city, besides which, Nicaragua refused to enter into any negotiations of this sort, and so the scheme petered out.

The first century of the Central American independence from Spain was celebrated in a fitting manner in Guatemala in 1921. To enter a new century of freedom in Central America, a meeting was called to form a federation of all the republics. The meeting was to take place in San José de Costa Rica. Nicaragua refused, because at that time she was actively engaged in a discussion with Costa Rica about boundaries. Guatemala, El Salvador, and Honduras entered into a union in 1921 with headquarters in Tegucigalpa, the capital of Honduras. Each one of the three above-named countries sent its representatives, and work was carried on for a while. In December, 1922, a revolution in Guatemala upset the scheme and once more the union failed. In 1934, the first Central American Conference was held in Guatemala City with the delegates from Guatemala, Honduras, and Nicaragua, who convened at the suggestion of President Dr. Juan Bautista Sacasa of Nicaragua. The discussions started amicably, though El Salvador and Costa Rica did not send delegates, as they had just declared that the Treaty of Peace and Amity signed in Washington in 1923 was null and void, and that they therefore had no need to attend any conference or to enter into any union. This was the last time an attempt was made to get together as one country.

Every one of the five republics realizes that a great future is in store for them if they could come to an understanding and enter into a union. Since the days of William Walker, Costa Rica has never taken kindly to the idea of a union. A union will eventually be achieved through an effort by one and all of these countries to stabilize on the same basic prin-

ciples their monetary systems and educational programs, to
remove their customs barriers, to provide good highways,
and to create a better understanding through publicity in
every section and every region of the five republics. Personal
ambitions and party differences must also be cast aside in
favor of a true spirit of cooperation and a desire for the
ultimate greatness of each and all of them as a whole, united
for mutual benefit and protection.

In synthesis, the above are the principal efforts to unite
the five Central American countries into one federation. On
the other hand, political parties in some of the countries
have used the standard of union as a cover for political
intrigues and revolts, which had little or nothing to do with
the union of Central America.

It is interesting to remark that an annexation was sought
by El Salvador with the United States of America, during
President Jackson's administration (1829-1837). This request
was refused by the latter country.

The Constitution of El Salvador provides in Article Six:
"El Salvador as a segregated part of the former Republic of
Central America, is authorized to assist with one or all of the
other states which formed that Republic, in the organization
of a National Government, when circumstances should per-
mit and the best interests of the country should require it."

In the modern history of El Salvador, General Manuel
Rivas Gómez, a Salvadorean by birth, might be said to have
been a living argument for a Federation of Central America. He was a popular figure in all five countries, wherein at
different times he managed to start unrest and revolutions.
He was named General de División of the armies in the five
Republics. He died in San Salvador in 1934.

MODERN EL SALVADOR

VIII

EL SALVADOR

THIS country, more than any of the other sister republics of Central America, has a definite fourth period in its history and development. Perhaps because of its constantly chaotic state, it has had to develop rapidly to keep abreast of the times. Since the start of this century, but particularly since 1921, a completely new era has commenced.

There is a slight discrepancy between the data regarding the area of the Republic of El Salvador: it is officially 34,126 square kilometers from the mouth of Rio Paz to the Gulf of Fonseca, including the islands in Jiguilisco Bay. Other figures give slightly less. In this territory there are about 2,193,425 inhabitants (Census of July, 1955); 3 percent are Indians and the rest are classified as *ladinos, mestizos,* and *criollos.* The present-day Indians are mixtures of the various Indian races of the first two periods in the history of this country (see page 11). The name *cheles* is given to foreigners, especially those with blue eyes and fair hair. The greater percentage of the foreigners come from Germany, Great Britain, France, and the United States. Mexico and the other Central American States have a large percentage of foreigners. There are very few, one could almost say no pure-blooded Negroes at the present time. Some Chinese have settled in the smaller towns where they are actively engaged in commerce.

GOVERNMENT

The government is vested in three chief authorities. As a democratic republican government it is presided over by the president, or executive power, assisted by eight ministers

53

and a number of undersecretaries. The president is elected by popular suffrage for a term of six years and must be over thirty-five years of age. He assumes office at midnight, September 14. He is also general commander of the armed forces. Two vice presidents *(designados)* are elected for one year.

The legislative power is vested in a National Assembly, composed of deputies and substitutes, elected by the people for a term of one year, with two ordinary sessions during the year, from February 15 to May 15, and from October 15 to January 2 of the next year, besides extraordinary sessions, when called by the executive and council of ministers. Three quarters of the total members of the Assembly form the quorum for a session. Congress has forty-two deputies, three from each of the fourteen departments, and starts its sessions punctually in the early part of February.

In every town and village, each year the decree for the election of the deputies to the Congress and for fixing the date for the presidential election must be read by *bandos* eight days before the day fixed in the decree for the election of the deputies.

The judicial power is vested in the Supreme Court of Justice and minor courts. El Salvador, as well as the other provinces in the Kingdom of Guatemala, was subject to the laws of Spain during the colonial era. By the Constitution of 1841, the judicial power was vested in the Supreme Court of Justice. The magistrates are elected for one year and may not be removed except for bad behavior.

The Constitution of 1886 was replaced by the modern one of 1950 now in force; it provides that the judicial power shall be exercised by the Supreme Court of Justice, the so-called *Cámeras de Segunda y Tercera Instancias,* and other dependent courts.

Salvadoreans are citizens by birth or naturalization. Those born in El Salvador, who are not declared citizens of another country by their foreign parents, are automatically recognized as Salvadoreans. Children of Central Americans born in El Salvador and those children of Salvadoreans born outside their country and inscribed in the respective Consulates are Salvadoreans.

The El Salvador woman has a right to vote and to be elected to office. When married to a foreigner she keeps her nationality unless she otherwise declares it, and she regains her nationality if divorced.

All foreigners are obliged to register with the police within twenty-four hours after entering the country.

The nomination of an individual during peacetime for military service is by lottery, according to the law. The permanent army during peacetime is annually fixed by the National Assembly and limited to the necessary number. Military men in active service do not have the right to vote, nor can they be elected to any post except the presidency.

Military service is obligatory for all Salvadoreans between the ages of eighteen and fifty. In case of war, all Salvadoreans are obliged to enter military service, and in peacetime Salvadoreans between the ages of eighteen and twenty-five years may be called for garrison duty.

Bandos are proclamations; an officer and a dozen or more soldiers station themselves at the principal corners of towns and villages and by the sound of a drum, attract attention of the population, and read a decree from the government, so that everybody may be informed. It is a survival of colonial procedure instituted for the illiterate, who thus have no excuse for disobeying a decree.

POLITICAL DIVISIONS

The Republic is divided into fourteen departments:

Department	*Capital of Department*
Santa Ana	Santa Ana
Ahuachapán	Ahuachapán
Sonsonate	Sonsonate
La Libertad	Nueva San Salvador
San Salvador	San Salvador
Chalatenango	Chalatenango
Cuzcatlán	Cojutepeque

La Páz	Zacatecoluca
San Vicente	San Vicente
Cabañas	Sensuntepeque
San Miguel	San Miguel
Usulután	Usulután
Morazán	San Francisco
La Unión	La Unión

The department of Cabañas was created by a legislative decree on February 10, 1873 and was named after the Central American, General Trinidad Cabañas, who distinguished himself under Francisco Morazán.

The Department of Cuzcatlán was created in 1835, and in 1855 was separated into the departments of Cuzcatlán and Chalatenango. In 1873 another piece was segregated and joined to the department of Cabañas.

The department of Morazán was created under the rule of General Santiago González as the result of an uprising in San Miguel in 1875.

Every department is ruled by a governor and a substitute nominated by the President. A *Comandante Departamental* (military ruler) appointed by the Minister of War is in charge of the garrisons and military equipment of every department.

A department is subdivided into *municipios* and these in turn are governed by a functionary appointed by the national administration. A board of aldermen, the number depending on the size of the *municipio,* assists the mayor *(alcalde)*.

CHIEFS OF STATE AND PRESIDENTS SINCE 1821

Jefe Político—Dr. Pedro Barrière	Sept.-Nov., 1821
Dr. Matías Delgado	1821-1823
Sr. Juan Manuel Rodríguez	1824
Supreme Chief—Juan Vicente Villacorta	1825-1826
José María Cornejo	1829-1830
José María Cornejo	1830-1832
Gen. Francisco Morazán	April-May, 1832
Mariano Prado	1832-1833

Provisional Chief—Gregorio Salazar   1834
           Joaquín Escalón   1834 (31 days)
Supreme Chief—Dionisio Herrera   1835
           Diego Vigil   1835-1837
           Gen. Grancisco Morazán   1839-1840
Provisional Chief—Norberto Ramírez   1840
           Juan Lindo   1841-1842
President—Dr. Juan J. Guzmán   April-June 1842
      Dr. Juan J. Guzmán   1842-1843
      Dr. Juan J. Guzmán   1843-1844
      Gen. Francisco Malespín   1844
      Joaquín E. Guzmán   1844-1845
      Dr. Eugenio Aguilar   1846-1848
      Doroteo Vasconcelos   1848-1850-1851
      Francisco Dueñas   1852-1853
      José María San Martín   1854
      José María San Martín   1854-1856
      Rafael Campo   1856-1858
      Miguel Santín   1858-1859
      Gen. Gerardo Barrios   1859-1860, 1861-1863
      Francisco Dueñas   1863-1865, 1871
      Gen. Sanitago González   1872-1876
      Andrés Valle   1876
      Rafael Zaldívar   1876-1885
      Gen. Fernando Figueroa   1885
      José Rosales   1885
Provisional President—Gen. Francisco Menéndez   1885-1886
Constitutional President—Gen. Francisco Menéndez   1886-1890
Provisional President—Carlos Ezeta   1890-1891
Constitutional President—Carlos Ezeta   1891-1894
Provisional President—Rafael Antonio Gutiérrez   1894-1895
Constitutional President—Rafael Antonio Gutiérrez   1895-1899
Provisional President—Tomás Regalado   1898-1899
Constitutional President—Tomás Regalado   1899-1903
      Pedro José Escalón   1903-1907
      Gen. Fernando Figueroa   1907-1911
      Dr. Manuel Enrique Araujo   1911-1913
Provisional President—Carlos Meléndez   1913-1914
      Dr. Alfonso Quiñónez M.   1914-1915
Constitutional President—Carlos Meléndez   1915-1918
Provisional President—Dr. Alfonso Quiñónez M.   1918-1919

Constitutional President—Jorge Meléndez   1919-1923
             Dr. Alfonso Quiñónez M.   1923-1927
             Dr. Pío Romero Bosque   1927-1931
             Ing. Arturo Araujo   1931
Vice President—Gen. Max. H. Martínez   1931-1934
Provisional President—Andrés I. Menéndez   1934-1935
Constitutional President—Max. H. Martínez   1935-1939, 1944
Provisional President—Osmín Aguirre Salines   1944-1945 [1]
Constitutional President—
      General Salvador Castaneda Castro   1945-1948
Junta Revolucionaria: 1948: Junta de Gobierno Mixta formada por: Teniento Coronel Oscar A. Bolaños, Dr. don Reynaldo Galinda Pohl, Dr. don Humberto Costa, Teniente Coronel Oscar Osorio, Teniente Coronel Jesús Córdoba; Reynaldo Galindo Pohl, Oscar Osorio, Manuel de Jesús Córdoba resigned and Oscar A. Bolaños and Dr. Humberto Costa remained at the head of the nation until 1950, when Teniente Coronel Oscar Osorio was elected constitutional president. His term ends in 1956.

The twentieth century in Central American political life has been distinguished by the long terms of office of some of the Presidents, including President Manuel Estrada Cabrera in Guatemala and President José Santos Zelaya in Nicaragua. In El Salvador, this twentieth-century system was really an oligarchy of the Meléndez-Quinónez family, which started in 1913, either as provisional Presidents or elected Presidents, and continued with one or another member of this family until 1927.

President Maximiliano H. Martínez started his presidential career in 1935 and remained in office until 1944, when a most unprecedented occurrence in the annals of Latin American history drove him into exile. A passive revolution took place, wherein all employees, both public and private, declared strikes (la huelga de los brazos caídos). During these nonresistant strikes every service was suspended, from hospital attendance to railroad traffic, and the

[1] The U.S.A. did not recognize the Aguirre regime until just before the Mexican Chapultepec Conference of Foreign Ministers of the Americas, which took place from February 21 to March 8, 1945. By that date elections had been held and General Salvador Castaneda Castro had been elected as President of the Republic. He took office on the first of March.

streets were filled with a sad and silent throng who thus passively protested the extension of the President's regime. By the end of April they had won their point, and immediately all services began functioning and life took on new vigor under a temporary regime prior to the calling of new elections and the convocation of an assembly to revise the constitution. A new constitution went into effect in 1950.

The National Flag and Coat of Arms

The first national flag that floated over San Salvador, a province of the Kingdom of Guatemala, was that of the Spanish Monarchy. The very brief annexation after the independence to Mexico substituted the Mexican flag and coat of arms for a very short time. When the republics of Central America formed the Federal Government under a united flag and coat of arms by a decree of the National Constitutional Congress of August 24, 1823, they adopted a new flag: two blue horizontal bars and one white, with a coat of arms in the middle of the white one. Once the Federation ended and each state became a separate nation, the General Assembly of the Republic of El Salvador on April 26, 1865, decreed a new flag, with nine horizontal blue and white stripes having nine stars at one corner to represent the then nine departments, which were replaced in 1912 by fourteen. On September 15, 1912, a new flag was adopted: the present one, three horizontal blue and white stripes with the coat of arms, which was changed at that time. The flag with coat of arms is allowed for official occasions only, and the ordinary flag with the same number of stripes does not have the coat of arms.

The national coat of arms was designed by Rafael Barraza Rodríguez and was officially established as such on May 17, 1912, during the administration of President Dr. Manuel Enrique Araujo. The background is somewhat similar to that of the coat of arms of the former Central American Federation.

The present one has in a triangle a mountain range with

five volcanoes arranged at the bottom on a background of water, bathed by the Atlantic and Pacific oceans. From this mountain range issues a Phrygian cap scattering light; between the rays in a semicircle are the words *15 Setiembre de 1921.*

At the back of the triangle there are five national flags, two at each side and one at the top. Underneath are inscribed the words: Dios Union Libertad (God, Union, and Liberty).

The national anthem music was composed by Don Juan Aberle, a well-known musician, and is considered one of the most harmonious national anthems in America. The words were written by the Salvadorean poet, Juan J. Cañas.

A legislative decree prohibits any foreign flag to float over buildings which are not those of the diplomatic representatives of other countries. When special permission is granted for nationals of other countries to hoist their own flags, it is with the understanding that no immunity is conceded to the person or home over which it floats.

LANGUAGE

The official language of the country is Spanish, although a few Indians still speak Nahuatl. Salvadoreans are good linguists, and most of the educated people speak several languages, particularly English, French, and German.

RELIGION

The country is predominantly Catholic, though all religious worship of whatever denomination is absolutely free and unmolested. Protestant missions are established in various parts of the country. The new Constitution of December 14, 1948, decreed the freedom of all religions in this country.

The Catholic Archbishop, who rules over the entire archdiocese, resides in San Salvador. San Miguel, Santa Ana, and San Vicente are bishoprics, each with a separate Bishop.

CLIMATE

According to the observations of the National Meteological Observatory, the following data are given:

Temperature in the shade

Mean temperature over entire year	23.6 C.
Extreme heat on April 9	26.9 C.
Minimum extreme January 21	10.6 C.
Mean maximum	33.6 C.
Mean minimum	15.0 C.

Rain in millimeters

Total for the year	1,645.1
Maximum in 24 hours—August 4	58.4
Number of days of perceptible rain	119
Number of days of imperceptible rain	19

Wind

Maximum velocity, January 19 and September 3	11.1
Dominant direction	N. and SSW.

Two well-defined seasons, the rainy and the dry season, aid vegetation in every sector of the country. The rainy season begins in May and ends in October, and the dry season covers the rest of the year. The best months of the year are December and January. The relative humidity is about 75 percent.

EDUCATION

The public school system is under the administration of the *Ministro de Cultura*.

The scholastic course is divided into kindergarten, six primary grades, five secondary grades, and four normal school grades, the latter having an additional year of practice for graduate teachers. After finishing the secondary schools, pupils may enter the National University, where they are taught branches *(Facultades)* of Jurisprudence and Social Sciences, Medicine and Surgery, Chemistry and Pharmacy, Architecture and Engineering, Economy, Odontology, the Humanities. The National University, now autonomous, was established by a decree of February 10, 1841, at the Convent of San Francisco, and now has large buildings of its own.

The figure for private schools is high because of the large number of Catholic denominational schools taught by nuns and priests. Primary education is compulsory for all inhabitants from the ages of seven to fourteen years. English, French, and Latin are included in the curriculum of the normal schools and in the Military Academy and higher academic courses. The *Jardín Infantil* and various kindergarten schools furnish preschool education for children from three to six years old.

Doctors, lawyers, chemists, and so forth, with university degrees are called "doctors," regardless of their profession. In other Central American countries only doctors and dentists are distinguished by this title, the others being titled *licenciados*.

Charities, Hospitals

Sixteen hospitals function in various parts of the country, besides those in the capital.[1]

Hospital Rosales in San Salvador is a large building well equipped with every modern convenience and apparatus. Doctors must give part of their time to work in the hospitals, and medical students practice during their last terms in this hospital.

Hospital Bloom, a children's hospital in San Salvador.
Sanatorio Nacional, San Salvador, for tubercular patients.

[1] An outstanding organization financed by the government and a citizens' organization is *Los Amigos de la Cuidad de Santa Ana,* established in 1950 for young delinquents. It is the *Ciudad de los Niños* (Boys' Town) which has done outstanding work.

Asilo Salvador, for the insane.
Hospital de Maternidad, opposite the Hospital Rosales.
Hospital San José, Chalchuapa.
Hospital Francisco Menéndez, Ahuachapán.
Hospital San Rafael, Santa Tecla.
Hospital Chalatenango, Chalatenango.
Hospital Cojutepeque, Cojutepeque.
Hospital San Vicente de Paul, Metapán.
Hospital de Oftalmia, San Salvador.
Hospital Santa Teresa, Zacatecoluca.
Hospital San Juan de Dios, San Miguel.
Hospital San José, Berlin (Department of Usulután).
Hospital de Jucuapa, (Department of Usulután).
Hospital La Unión, La Unión.
Hospital San Juan de Dios, Santa Ana.
Hospital Sonsonate, Sonsonate.
Hospital Sensuntepeque.
Hospital Regalado in San Salvador (under construction).
Casa de Salud Santa Florentina, Santiago María.
Asilo Santa Narcisa, Santa Ana.
Asilo Sara for the aged and blind, founded by the wife of ex-President Rafael Zaldívar.
The Military Hospital in San Salvador is a well-organized institution.

The larger coffee cleaning establishments and factories have established the *Sala Cunas* annexed to the main building, where children of working women are lodged and fed during the day. This provides modern sanitation for children while their mothers work.

The *Sala Cuna Temporal* (Temporary Crêche) was instituted by the Lions Club for the purpose of caring for children whose mothers are temporarily interned in hospitals.

The *Sociedad Pro Infancia* is a group of individuals who are interested in studying ways to better the diet and care of children and to cut down the enormous mortality among children under five years of age.

The *Instituto de la Vivienda Rural and Instituto para Colonización Rural del Campó* are outstanding institutions for the benefit of the population. They are directed primarily toward distributing small tracts of land among the people to create small independent farms. They also provide housing projects for the workmen in rural centers.

La Gota de Leche is a charity institution where poor mothers are provided with daily rations of milk for their small children.

El Salvador is notable in Latin America for its endeavors to promote the public welfare. The center of this work is the office of the *Beneficencia Pública* with branches in most departments. The new and very modern building of the *Sanidad Pública* has the necessary laboratories for modern investigation. Most of the work in the last few years has centered around the sanitation problem in those areas where an enormous percentage of deaths was due to malaria.

This department, in collaboration with the Department of Coordination of Inter American Affairs (U.S.A.) has had spectacular success in the districts where malaria has been particularly prevalent, reducing the percentage from 90 to 50 in such areas as San Miguel and Sonsonate. Swamps have been scientifically drained and concrete drainage canals have prevented the muddy overflow of the waters. This has served a double purpose: it has killed the malaria-bearing Anopheles mosquito, and has made new tracts of land available for agriculture.

There are several *Casas de Salud,* where paying patients are received and attended by the doctors who own these private hospitals.

The Orphan Asylum and *El Buen Pastor* are managed by nuns. The latter is an admirable institution in San Salvador, where wayward girls are interned and taught practical cooking, laundry work, fine sewing, and embroidery by the nuns.

The School for the Blind in Santa Ana was established and is supported by the Lions Club.

The Vocational School in San Salvador *(La Escuela Vocacional)* is an up-to-date institution.

Holidays

Officially recognized holidays for the country are:

January 1, New Year's Day
Holy Week from Wednesday
Every six years, inauguration of the President on September 14
July 24 to August 6, Feast of *El Salvador del Mundo* with holidays from August 1 to August 6
September 15, Central American Independence
October 12, *Día de la Raza* (Columbus Day)
November 5, commemorating the first Cry of Independence
December 25, Christmas Day
December 31, Bank Holiday

Several lesser celebrations commemorate outstanding achievements and there are many religious holidays, which are punctually observed.

Magazines, Newspapers

These are in the Spanish language; the government official publication is *El Diario Oficial.*

In 1824 the Congress and the patriot, Juan Manuel Rodríguez, launched the first important press in El Salvador. Rodríguez donated a press with its accessories to print the legislative and executive orders and established a paper, *Primer Periódico Semanario Político Mercantil.*

In 1844 President General Francisco Malespín brought out the first number of the *Gaceta Oficial del Gobierno de la Confederación Centro Americana.*

The principal present-day newspapers are *El Diario Latino, El Diario de Hoy, Patria Nueva, La Prensa Gráfica, La Tribuna Libre,* and *El Heraldo de Sonsonate. El Diario de Occidente,* published in Santa Ana, is the oldest newspaper in the country. Newspapers are also published in San Miguel, Sonsonate, Usulután, Ahuacphapán, and San Vicente.

COMMUNICATIONS

Domestic and foreign radio and cable communications are maintained throughout the country by the All America Cable Company, with offices in *El Palacio de Comunicaciones* in San Salvador City.

Telegraph communication covers every part of the country; international telegraphic and telephone communications are government institutions with central offices in San Salvador.

El Salvador is a member of the Pan American Postal Union, and except for air mail postage every letter must have the regular eight-cent (Salvador) postage.

TRANSPORTATION

Railways—International Railroads of Central America (I. R. C. A.) connect El Salvador with Guatemala and thence to the Mexican frontier at Ayutla. From the Atlantic port of Puerto Barrios in Guatemala, 459 kilometers of railroad in this country connect the Guatemala frontier at Angiatú with the Bay of Fonseca at Puerto Cutuco.

The El Salvador Railroad Company is owned by British capital. It has 145 kilometers of road which connect the capital with the port of Acajutla.

Airways—All international and well-known companies have daily planes north and south, connecting with Eastern Airlines in the U.S.A., and with Canadian Airlines, Air France, K.L.M., Mexican lines, and South American lines. TACA, a Salvadorean firm, flies from New Orleans.

Steamships—Trade and passenger steamer services connect the northern and southern hemispheres and European countries.

Roads—The country is traversed by paved roads that connect the principal towns with the capital. All villages and towns of even small importance are connected with the capital of their department by fairly good roads.

The Pan American Highway, El Salvador Section—From its beginning at the Guatemalan frontier the Pan American Highway is completely paved and passes through densely populated regions. From the bridge over the Guascorán River (the boundary between El Salvador and Honduras), stretches a superb panorama of volcanic groups of formidable active cones. This highway crosses the Lempa River over a great bridge four hundred meters long and forty meters wide. Forty-eight kilometers from the city of San Miguel this paved road has a branch to La Unión (six kilometers), and from this junction it is only thirty-eight kilometers to the abovementioned river, where it crosses into Honduras. The road branches to the capital of that country (Tegucigalpa) and then proceeds to Nicaragua.

Sports and Recreation

Riding—Trails crisscross the country. Both men and women ride horseback, especially the owners of plantations, where riding is a necessity to supervise their properties. Races are held during the August holidays, and there is keen competition among the owners of thoroughbred stock and also in the Plaza Conchalita, especially used by the working class.

Bicycling and motorcycling are favorite sports. Salvadoreans are adepts at swimming—in inland pools, rivers, and at the seashore. Baseball, football, and basketball games are well attended. Central America holds Olympic Games every four years with athletes from the five republics, Mexico, Pánama, and the Caribbean Islands attending. Tennis is played at the various sport clubs in San Salvador as well as at the Campo de Marte; there are sport clubs in the various departments and good golf courses at the Country Club and at other sports clubs.

Fishing for marlin, pike, and large fish of other varieties is popular in the Gulf of Fonseca and all along the seacoast. Smaller fish, lobsters, and game fish are abundant, while alligator hunting is a wonderful sport in the less populated water ways.

IX

THE SALVADOREAN PEOPLE

THE three different eras in the history of El Salvador have left their definite imprints on the people. Very distinct social strata are at present perceptible: the higher class people, the middle class, who have appeared as a factor in the social environment during the last twenty-five years, and the enormous percentage we may consider as a lower class. The Indians are such a negligible factor nowadays that we do not have to consider them in this résumé.

Women—To sew a fine seam, to sit on a tufted cushion, and to have a gay time was literally the pattern of life of a highborn Salvadoreña until a decade ago. Filled with prejudices inherited from their colonial forefathers, young girls and young matrons kept strictly to the old tradition that women should be purely decorative, and they were waited on by numerous handmaids, so that their pristine beauty might not be marred by any work or worry. They were carefully escorted by chaperons to the fiestas which, whether private or in the clubhouses, were brilliant gatherings. The chaperons were seated against the walls, and let nothing escape their eagle eyes.

Salvadoreans travel extensively, so that gradually it became fashionable to send the girls to Europe to be educated. Later the United States also became popular. When she came home, the young maid stoutly declared her right to go out into the world and forage for herself on an equal footing with her brothers. She was urged to desist, for no socially minded young person admitted to the innermost sanctuary of society should be allowed to *work* (horrible word). Working for a living was unheard of, when father and brothers were willing, nay, delighted to maintain her in the way her forefathers thought suitable until a husband came along. But she insisted, having other ideas than marrying the first to come along who offered heart and board, so she found herself a job, dressed in the latest styles, and calmly walked out on her board of council to take that job. To the amazement of her family and friends, she held down that job in a manner quite fitting to a graduate of a good school and business course in the U.S.A.

In the afternoons after business was over, she drove her own car and gathered her friends for a set of tennis or a swim and picnic at La Libertad beach, and thus set the example for other girls. Astounded parents helplessly watched as their chicks followed these first steps in the emancipation of women. At the present time an efficient set of young people work in offices, stores, and even such institutions steeped in old tradition as the University and graduate schools have opened their doors to ambitious girls. Notwithstanding her efficient work, the Salvadorean girl manages to grace all festivities of a social nature and distinguishes herself at all sorts of sports. She is also much interested in the various branches of the arts, and manages to find time to develop her inherent talent. Her dress is no longer the latest style worn in Paris, but she has adopted the more serviceable American business model, which looks so smart and trim on the Salvadorean woman.

The women of the middle class also work and are educated side by side with their sisters from the social élite. Nowadays there is scarcely a perceptible difference in the two classes, and despite inhibiting tradition, modern ways and education will very soon overstep the invisible line that separates the two classes.

The working women of the third class, with their part-Indian backgrounds, have from time immemorial been expected to work and contribute to the household income. In the whole world there are no more hard-working and industrious individuals than the women of this class. Dressed in simple frocks of cotton, with their baskets filled with a variety of articles, they sit on street corners and earn a modest income by selling cigarettes, candy, paper flowers, and other articles made with their own hands in their poverty-stricken homes.

These women live with their menfolk in community houses called _mesones_, or in small houses on the outskirts of the cities and towns. The birth rate is enormously high, and the mortality among children is shocking. Their living standard is low and their economic buying power is almost nil. Despite all this, they seem to thrive and enjoy life according to their standards. Religious pageants and church festivities are their main entertainments, supplemented in more recent times by motion pictures.

This third class is the backbone of the country. They are never idle a minute, and take advantage of every opportunity to make a few cents. On feast days their baskets are filled with edibles for the crowds that line the streets. At nightfall they sit beside portable stoves and cook _pupusas_ (large corn-paste cakes filled with delicious cream cheese), which must be eaten very hot, directly from the clay dish on which they have been roasted; or they prepare steaming hot coffee mixed with heaps of sweet black sugar and served in clay cups, or they serve _atole_, a drink made from ground corn.

Upper-class women now manage their own estates when the need arises. Young people dance unchaperoned in sophisticated evening costumes in the modern clubhouses, and talk in many languages to their partners as they discuss world affairs to the latest dip and turn of modern dances. The modern girl is a woman of the world equally at home in London, New York, or China, and thinks nothing of rushing over to Mexico, Guatemala, or Panama for a week-end to help her husband race his blooded horses, or buy a few new frocks and jewels.

Supercosmopolitan is the word to apply to the modern Salvadorean woman who takes everything in her stride.

Men—The upper-class men who were accustomed to traveling all over the globe before the recent world chaos made it
their habit to leave the country after the profitable coffee
crop had been garnered to undertake extensive tours of
Europe, which were prolonged until the next crop required
their attention at home. Nowadays traveling has been cur-
tailed, and the money that formerly flowed out of the
country is now freely spent at home in improving estates,
building modern and comfortable houses, and in helping
generously in every branch of public welfare.

The best type of Salvadorean man loves sports and is
adept at all of them. Blooded cattle, race horses, special
breeds of dogs are within his field of interest. He is pleasure-
loving and gay, and never misses an opportunity to celebrate.
The professional men are outstanding in their fields. Several
of the younger generation fly their own planes, and in general keep up with the times and events of the world.

The second class is industrious, hard-working, and endeavoring to forge ahead. In this class intellectual ambition
is growing rapidly.

The lower class still has a very small stake in the financial
resources of the country. Formerly it provided more than
enough manpower for every branch of agriculture and industry, and even now it is a strong bulwark for agricultural
activities. The men of this class work from sunup to sun-
down.

Strange to say, the poorer class is not in the main illiterate,
and therefore newspapers have a rather stronger influence
on the masses than in most of the other countries of Central
America.

Every one of them, women as well as men, of the three
classes are lovable people, high strung, perhaps even more
patriotic than other people on this continent, self-satisfied
and contented with their lot. The stranger within their gates
finds this country and its people a pleasant adventure.

X

PRESENT-DAY INDIANS

THE INDIAN POPULATION

AT A high estimate, but 3 percent of the total population may be classified as Indians: that is to say, descendants of the Indian races, who settled in this country and at least preserved part of their traditions, language, and dress. Others, though not officially classified as Indians, because they have adopted the dress and manners of the *ladinos,* are truly more Indian than otherwise in every way.

In many villages the Indians have adopted a costume that accords with the warm climate. Thus the descendants of the Lenca and those Nahuatls of the Costa del Bálsamo, despite having changed their dress fashions, are still Indians at heart and preserve some of their traditions. Panchimalco, Izalco, and Nahuizalco are the best places wherein to study the present-day Nahuatl Indians, because they still preserve some of their costumes, crafts, traditions, and customs, as well as the remnants of their language and music.

THE NEGROID ADMIXTURE

The racial history of this country is complicated; there is another race that settled and left descendants among the Indians and white men. In 1541 by royal decree African Negroes were brought to work in the mines and *factorias,* the indigo and sugar plantations. They multiplied and their strain was mixed with the Indian despite strict prohibition. In early colonial days the mixture of Negro and Indian was considered the lowest in the social scale, looked down upon

72

by both the Indians and the Negroes. The Negroes settled particularly in the region of Zacatecoluca, San Vicente, and Chinameca. They were able to withstand admirably the intense heat of some of these regions, and therefore were splendid workers in many arduous tasks.

At the present day the descendant of either Negro and white man or Negro and Indian is generally known as *mulato*, though there was a time when the word *mulato* was also applied to the admixture of white and Indian. Nowadays Negroes are known as *morenos*, though only few of the descendants of the true Negroes of the early colonial days remain in this country. The general name *ladino* is applied to the descendants of Negro and white, as also to the Indian and white admixture, though the latter are in reality *mestizos*, and the word *ladino* is erroneously applied to all the white people, who should be known as *criollos*. *Ladino* is properly applied to persons having 80 to 90 percent other race mixtures with the Indian. Acculturation has taken place so thoroughly that now it is impossible to classify clearly the different racial groups.

INDIAN LIFE

The Indian lives in a thatched hut, with one or two rooms, wherein the family sleep, cook, and carry on their crafts, if any. Depending upon where the Indian village is situated, the thatch roof is small or may extend almost to the ground, thus providing a cool refuge from the sun. A special room is reserved in the house of one of the principal men for the altar of the saint or saints of the village. This room is called *cofradía*, and therein ceremonies and special festivities are held at various dates during the year. The date on which the patron saint's day of the village is celebrated is of great significance, and the saint is taken with due ceremony for a visit to the village church. The *cofrades* are men who are elected to this post because of their descent, wealth, or good standing in the community. (The name *cofradía* is of Spanish derivation.) These men have charge of everything connected with the *cofradía;* sometimes more than one *cofradía* is found in the larger villages, where several saints are worshiped.

It is not difficult to furnish a hut. Usual equipment includes a mat *(petate)* that is rolled up and stored in the rafters during the day, or a rude wooden bedstead with a mat instead of a mattress over the hide thongs, and a gaily colored cotton sheet; a bench or perhaps a chair, in one corner a table or altar whereon the picture or image of a saint is placed amid decorations of paper flowers, and lighted candles if the day is a holiday. One corner of the hut or an outside corridor is reserved as a kitchen. This is the most lively place, as all day the charcoal fire is alight and over it clay pots precariously balance against one another. This stove is placed upon a tablelike arrangement of four sticks on which hard clay and mud have been combined to make a good support for the fire. No ovens are used, but sometimes there is a special section for baking outside the hut, or a small village may own a community beehive-shaped oven, wherein festive bread is baked. There is always a large basket to wash the corn. Most important of all to the Indian cook is the *metate* or grinding stone. These grinding stones are different in this country from those of the *ladinos,* and also from those used in some other countries. They are really more like those found in pre-Columbian ruins in the North, made from stone placed on a tablelike elevation with two supports, and hollowed much more than the usual *metate.* On the *metate* most of the food is ground: chile peppers, corn, tomatoes, cocoa, coffee, or anything else that helps to flavor the food.

Dried corn husks are a great help to the Indian cook, who uses them in different ways; bananas wrapped in corn husks and cooked are delectable bits. Corn paste *tamales* are wrapped in corn husks, and dried corn husks also serve to clean the kitchen utensils.

Food—The Indians' specialty is corn, particularly the *tortillas* or round cakes made of corn paste, and cooked on a flat clay dish or *comal*. They take the place of our bread. Black beans, *frijoles*, are universally used among both the Indians and the lower-class *ladinos*. They have an occasional bit of meat, when it is possible to obtain it, preferably meat of wild animals. They eat vegetables in small quantities, and many kinds of chile peppers to flavor the food. Coffee is sweetened with black sugar and fruit. It must be emphasized that corn and dishes made out of corn, as well as drinks from corn either fermented or combined with chocolate, chile, or other spices, together with black beans, form the basic food.

The drink called *chicha* is fermented corn, made by grinding the corn and placing it in an earthenware pot covered with water, then heating to the boiling point. The froth is decanted and the grain left to ferment. After forty-eight hours, it is again decanted and placed in a clay jug with brown sugar and maguey fruit, and left to ferment for another period. During the first fermentation, lasting from three to four days, this beverage is tasty, but afterward the alcoholic content is raised 5 to 8 percent and it is exceedingly intoxicating.

Just as in olden times, corn is the leit motiv that runs through Indian life. If the crops are good, the Indians are prosperous. If times are bad, they go hungry. At least a dozen different kinds of beverages and food concoctions are made with corn as the basic ingredient.

To the casual observer, the Indians present a good Christian front, and worship devotedly in the village church. On the other hand, they appease their deities by offerings of candles and flowers in well-known caves or on stone altars by the wayside. They are superstitious: not many years ago, at the summer soltice, Indians from all over the country gathered near the crater of the San Salvador volcano, and there carried on ceremonies to pacify its spirit, which had wrought so much havoc upon the people living in these lands. Offerings were of fowls and turkeys, and it is whispered that long ago a child bedecked with flowers was thrown into the maw of the monster. Ceremonies at Lake Ilopango similar to the ones just mentioned were also carried out. Nowadays, these ceremonies are reduced to offerings of fruit, flowers, and turkeys, with much incense, so the Indians feel sure that they have complied with their duty.

They believe in omens, and have some strange beliefs and practices such as, for example, women carrying large bunches of *ruda* in the procession celebrating the festival of the patron saint in the village of Panchimalco, *El Corazón de Jesús* (Heart of Jesus). As it was explained, this herb would be beneficial in combating heart ailments. In Izalco, the "Fiesta de la Cruz" is celebrated in front of the largest cross, *Cruz Galante;* this is by no means a Christian ceremony, as it is punctiliously dated for the planting of the principal corn crop in May.

The hot springs near town are not used by the Indians, because "these waters are boiled inside the volcano and have been used by the presiding deities to cook and wash their clothes." For the Izalco Indians the moon is represented by the rabbit, imagined as playfully leaping from east to west. They claim to discern a picture of a rabbit in the moon, and believe that the moon influences the ocean and all waters. When the sun is very red it is having a fight with the moon; then the women take their gourds filled with water and make a great noise to help the moon, and the men join with their musical instruments to help the sun.

The Izalco Indians are most superstitious; when a woman is pregnant, she must not look at the moon during an eclipse. However, should she place an obsidian knife in her belt, the moon will not injure the baby. Should she neglect this precaution, the baby will surely be imperfect. The moon governs the rainy season, and the sun the dry season. The moon regulates the woman's periods. The woman's life is completely governed by the moon myths, which are endless. Near this village, on a hill called Anicoyotl, rites were formerly celebrated in honor of the God of Rain, Tlaloc. This rain deity is still invoked to provide the proper weather for the crops.

The present-day Indians in the southern region still use

the same weapons for hunting as their forefathers. Bows and arrows are made out of the wood of the *Huiscoyol* tree, and have three distinct kinds of arrows. These arrows formerly were also used instead of bayonets. Gay bird feathers and the seeds of a tree known as *Lágrimas de San Pedro* trim the arrows. Half a dried gourd placed so as to protect the hand is part of the bow.

Until recently, the fishermen employed *barbasco*, which they placed in the waters of the rivers. This powerful poison killed the fish, which were then netted by the fishermen standing in convenient narrows, where a dam of sticks and leaves had been placed in the river. This poisoning procedure not only killed the larger fish which serve as food, but also destroyed eggs and young fish wherever the poisonous waters touched; so in 1933 a law was passed prohibiting the use of *barbasco*. It is the root of a plant known as *camotillo* (curcuma tintoria, zingiberaciae) mixed with lime. This was the most used poison, though it was sometimes replaced by the leaves of the añil (indigofera suffruticosa) and the roots of other poisonous plants. These roots as well as other parts of plants and leaves were mashed before being put into the water. This was a hereditary custom in which all the family participated, particularly during the week before Holy Week, when fish is in general the food used all over the country.

XI

COSTUMES AND CRAFTS

Costumes

THE majority of the Indian men wear white cotton trousers, one or both legs rolled to the knee. A white shirt hangs loosely to the thigh, gathered into a square yoke and with long sleeves, which are usually rolled to the elbow. A large palm leaf hat with a high crown, a staff to help him on his journey over rough trails, and sandals with thongs to hold them complete his costume. Occasionally the shirt is tucked into the trousers, and a red belt or sash is wound around his middle. A string net to hold any merchandise or produce carried to market is also an adjunct.

The women's costumes vary according to the section of the country where they are worn. The old traditional costumes are seldom seen, except in the villages of Panchimalco, Izalco, and Nahuizalco. The Indians of Panchimalco wear enormously wide gathered skirts, one end tucked into the waist, to show a white petticoat trimmed with a lace or embroidered ruffle. The skirt literally drags on the ground and is finished off at the edge with a wide ruffle, which adds yards to the *enaguilla*. The material is cotton, in tiny dark blue and red checks. It is trimmed around the hips with cross-stitch or smocking in colored thread—a unique garment, reminiscent of the wide skirts used by the Spanish ladies of the sixteenth and seventeenth centuries.

The blouse or *huipil* is never handwoven nowadays; it is a plain, bright-colored cotton blouse with ruffles at the neck, a yoke, and short puffed sleeves. It is trimmed with store-bought lace, embroidery, tucks, or shirring, sometimes arranged to simulate some sort of yoke. The only handwoven part of the costume is the square cloth that covers the baskets or wraps around the food. Two long braids are thrown over the shoulders and finished off with strips of cloth or ribbon. The head is covered by a large bright cotton cloth, which hangs down the back. Formerly this was also handwoven.

The *refajos* or skirts worn in Izalco and Nahuizalco are of the tightly wrapped around variety, obliging the wearer to squat and not to sit. These *refajos* are similar to those worn by the Indians in the Guatemala highlands. True to tradition, these Indians buy theirs only from traders, who appear once a year. The skirt must be made from the standard five-yard length of fabric. The Nahuizalco *refajo* is never bought from traders; it is woven locally in some village where the weaving is carried on on foot looms. This difference between the two neighboring and allied villages is strictly observed. The belt worn by the Izalco women, also reminiscent of the belts used in some regions of Guatemala, is a distinction of these women, who considered themselves above the plebeian Nahuizalcos. Whether this has anything to do with the account that the Nahuatl people were captained by chiefs of the Maya race when they arrived in this region, or whether there is any connection with the latter-day Guatemala Indian trade, I cannot say. The above-mentioned belt is woven on the primitive hip-strap hand loom, and *seda floja* of Chinese silk, in bright colors, is usually used for its decorations, although nowadays twisted silk is sometimes employed.

The *huipil* or blouse in both these villages is like most of those worn in the rest of the country. A love of color prevails, and the cotton materials are of the brightest blue, pink, red, or yellow, with self-colored trimmings on the cotton material.

In various parts of the country the women wear long chemiselike white cotton garments, which fall over the scanty skirt, neither one or the other having any trimmings. Some women wear *rebozos* or *perrajes*. These shawls are not the rule, but rather the exception. They are woven on foot

looms or bought from traders, and serve admirably to cover
the head and hang loose in a typical manner down the back
of the wearer. Most of these shawls are in dark blue with a
few black or white stripes, finished off with knotted fringes
at both ends.

The women also wear sandals, as a great many of the villages are on hills rough to climb. The jewelry consists of a
rosario (rosary). It is not very long and has many colored untwisted silk rosettes placed between the silver coins and
beads that make up the rest of the chain. The silver figures,
which hang from this chain, are made of tiny flat pieces of
silver, like paper dolls. The cross at the end is of heavy silver and well rounded. Another kind of *rosario* is made of
red or green silk threads studded with dried palm seeds. In
Panchimalco, a small scapulary hangs at the end of either
kind of rosary. The *Corazón de Jesús* (The Heart of Jesus)
is embroidered neatly on a piece of cloth and is displayed
prominently on the front of the *camisa* or *huipil*. Modern
beads have taken the place of the long coin *chachal* formerly
worn by most of the Indians. Brass or silver rings set with
colored stones are sometimes worn, as well as silver or gold
earrings, but there does not seem to be much pride among
them as to the jewelry they possess.

A basket is an inseparable adjunct to a woman's ensemble
—by no means the ones with handles, but a flat well-woven
basket having a few strands of color to liven the effect. It is
usually balanced on the head over the shawl or head ker-
chief.

Ladino Costumes—The women of the *ladinos* (the greater
part of Indian race mixtures), are *mengalas;* they wear skirts,
enaguas, and *blusas*—a cross between modern clothes and
their own adaptations. Usually the *blusa* is trimmed with
lace and embroidery around sleeves and neck, and tucked
into a very wide pleated cotton *enagua,* trimmed with a
few ruffles around the bottom. It reaches to the ankles. The
skirt is worn over some kind of petticoat, *fustán,* and held
up around the waist by a cotton or silk belt—or often no belt

is worn. Others wear an adapted cotton one-piece costume, in reality more or less a fitted Mother Hubbard costume. Chains of colored beads are worn around the neck and a cotton shawl, *rebozo,* which varies according to the region, completes the costume. The hair is worn in two braids down the back. The men wear the white cotton costume with trousers more on the modern style than those of the true Indians, and usually made out of some material of a better wearing quality. Their hats, though with a broad brim, do not have as high a crown as the true Indian hats. Shoes take the place of sandals.

Textiles

The spinning of fibers from vines and fibrous leaves was practiced long before cotton was woven into textiles. At the present time most of the textiles woven and worn in this country are of cotton, which grows plentifully in all regions.

The primitive method of spinning has entirely vanished. A few spin and weave in Panchimalco and belts are woven in Izalco. In this process the cotton is cleaned and prepared for the spindle, a stick about half a yard long with a clay or wood whorl at its lower end, four or five inches from the point. When in use, this implement rests the pointed end in a gourd or large seashell. The woman squats on the ground and rapidly turns the spindle with one hand while feeding the raw cotton with the other. Now the cotton is ready for the reel and warping bar. In the above-mentioned villages complicated gadgets have been discarded, and the cotton is wound on small pegs planted in the ground at the required distance for the loom. Cotton and the untwisted silk used for the belts are prepared by a woman who holds one end of the skein of silk or cotton with her big toe, and elevates the other end of the thread above her shoulder with her hand, while she deftly manipulates it to the required length for the warp.

The loom, of the same pre-Columbian type, is composed of sticks, the number of these depending on the technique used for the textile. One end of the loom is anchored by a band around the waist or buttocks of the weaver, and the other to a rafter or branch of a tree. The weaver has smaller sticks wound with variously colored threads, which serve her as shuttles. It is amazing how quickly and deftly the weaver achieves either the plain or more complicated technique.

The ancient hip-strap hand loom is now being supplanted by the foot looms, which are worked by *ladinos,* more often in *talleres* (workshops) where several men do the work than as a home industry. An enormous trade has been developed in the textiles woven on foot looms, and the quality and color schemes are commendable.

For these looms the cotton is bought ready in strands (*madejas*), bargained by the pound, and in most cases already dyed in the required colors. A mechanized reel, warping bar, and other implements for this work are employed. The looms resemble the pre-Jacquard type, first introduced by the Spanish colonials.[1] Later-day adaptations have been made on them. At the present time large factories are established wherein weaving is done by the most modern and up-to-date methods and machinery. They supply the greater part of the demand for cotton materials, but of course these are entirely different from the ones mentioned above, which are still to be found in regions of Indian or part-Indian population, and where the more primitive loom of colonial days is still in vogue.

DYEING

Before mentioning the splendid vegetable, mineral, and animal dyes formerly used by the Indians, it is well to emphasize that at the present time aniline dyes have with a few exceptions taken their place. The following are a few that are still known:

Blue—Indigo (*añil*), important in colonial days as well as at the present. This country has always been a famed center

1 The Jacquard loom was invented by Joseph Marie Jacquard in France, about 1804. It is distinguished by special cards for weaving patterns on the cloth.

for indigo. The best known are *Sacatinta* and *Jiquilite,* of which there are several varieties; all grow in abundance, particularly in the valleys of the region of San Vicente. The leaves are washed in hot water and thoroughly mashed. The residue is gathered into a large clay jar or wooden tub with water and lye.

The *Sacatinta* variety (Fuchsia parviflora Zirec: Onacgraceae) grows profusely on the slopes of the volcanoes of San Salvador and San Vicente. Another variety, Jacobinia specigera (Schlecht) Bailey (Gesneriaceae), commonly known as *Hierba de la Santísima Trinidad, Hierba de Santa Inez,* or *Tinta,* is also employed by laundresses for bluing clothes. When mixed with different acids, this dye turns reddish. The most common varieties of *Jiquilite* are Indigofera guatemalensis (Mociño y Sessé—Fabaccea), having small straight pods, and Indigofera suffruticosa Farbaceae, with large curved pods. The first named grows plentifully in the departments of San Vicente and Chalatenango, the latter in San Miguel. Blue is also extracted from the *irayol* or *guaitil* plant (Genipa americana).

Black—The fruit of the *Nacascolo* (Caesalpinia coriaria: Caesalpinaceae) tree is the principal source for this color for all crafts. The fruit is well mashed and boiled in a solution previously prepared and allowed to ferment, made with black loaf sugar, dissolved in water, to which a handful of rusty nails is added. Some overripe *marañón* fruit is also mixed into the dye pot, which is called *tinaco.* First the cotton thread is submerged in the dye pot, then allowed to dry for several days. Then it is dipped into the second dye pot, and when the desired color is achieved, the cotton is rinsed in clear water. This fruit of the *Nacascolo* is not to be confused with Nascacolo (Pithecolobium pachypus: mimosacea); this name is used in San Salvador, and *Guachimol* in Sonsonate, a plant from which writing ink was formerly extracted.

The *Terminalia catapa* gives a deep black dye. This tree was originally imported from India. The bush known as

Espino blanco (Acacia cultriformis—Mimosaceae) has a large percentage of tannin and is sometimes used for black dye; the exact shade of black depends on the mineral combined with the dye plants.

Rushes are dyed black with a mixture of black roasted coffee and the liquid extracted from the *Mashaste* plant. Strands for hat weaving are buried in the ground until thoroughly discolored by the soil into black. For gourds, two dye pots are prepared: *La Tinta* in the first with the boiled Nacascolo fruit, in the second a solution of fermented corn (called *chicha*), water, and oxidized nails.

Brown—For light brown, the skin of the *nance* (Brysonima crassifolia L.: Malpighiaceae) fruit is used. Dark brown is obtained from the bark of the *Aliso* tree, (Alnus acuminata) (Betulaceae), belonging to the alder family.

The *Mashaste* or *Majaste* is a woody vine with mauve flowers and reddish leaves, and a favorite for dyeing the reeds for baskets, hat palm leaves, and for mats. The leaves, when ripe, are a deep red color, and when boiled with the above-mentioned materia prima, give off a reddish brown dye.

Red—A great source of wealth during the colonial period was the red dye extracted from the cochineal bug. This grows wherever cacti are plentiful. It is the best red dye for coloring textiles.

The *Annatto* tree (Bixa Orellana L. Bixaceae)—*achiote*—has a fruit that supplies a good red dye, as well as one of a yellowish color. The common name Brazil is given to different species of dye woods, mostly red dye. The bark is used of different kinds of trees with the general names *Sangre de Toro, Brasil, Tiñecanastos,* which come under the classification of *Palo de Brasil* or *Palo Amarillo* (Chlorophora tinctoria: Moraceae). Other varieties are known as *Campeche* (Haemtoxylon campechianum: Caesalpinoideae), *Drago,* and *Sangre de Chucho.* This latter bark gives a rose color. There is also a species of the *Brasil* which gives forth a colorless liquid that turns red when it comes in contact with air.

Yellow—Orange-yellow is extracted from the *Camotillo* (Curcuma tinctoria: Zingiberaceae), and reddish-yellow from the above-mentioned *Achiote* fruit. A bright yellow is extracted from the root of the *Cabello de Angel,* mixed with indigo, water, and lye.

Purple—The *Chlorophora tinctoria* is used for this color, mixed with different minerals.

For setting colors, the leaves of the *Tempate* bush (Jatropha Curcas L.: Euphorbiaceae) are mashed, and the liquid is added to the cotton or materia prima for weaving hats, mats, and baskets, after they are colored with the dye, and also the leaves of the *Cinco Negritos* (Lanta Camara, L. Verbenaceae).

Silk, when obtainable, and wool are never dyed.

FIBER CRAFT

Though the craft of weaving textiles has become almost extinct in this country, other crafts have forged ahead, and are indispensable to the economic life of the Indians and lower-class *ladinos.* The fiber, mat and hat weaving, basket making, and ceramic crafts of this country are outstanding in Central America.

The fiber weaving craft is well developed. String, rope, bags, pack animal accessories, the famous hammocks, slings for casting stones, saddlebags, and other useful adjuncts are easily obtained at minimum prices.

The fibers of the henequen, and many varieties of the Agnus genus (Amarilidacenae) such as maguey, sisal, mescal, *mezcalito* (Manila Hemp), *abaca* (Musa textiles), *pitón* and *pita floja,* as well as the *escobilla* (Sida rhombifolia L. Malvaceae) (teasel), are frequently used for rope and for weaving bags. It is estimated that a rope of henequen, measuring twelve and a half millimeters in circumference, resists or can sustain a weight of four hundred pounds. The principal region for henequen cultivation is the San Miguel sector. Most of the fiber from this area is either exported or used commercially in the large modern factories where coffee bags and other articles are woven.

Rude looms of various kinds are employed in the fiber crafts. The Lenca Indians use looms one and a half yards long by one yard wide to weave pack-animal accessories, slings, and saddlebags of untwisted fiber (*pitón*), which is much coarser than the other fibers mentioned.

Hammocks are woven by stretching warp fibers on a large horizontal wood frame at a slight elevation from the ground. A man throws the shuttle with the weft string across the frame through the warp fibers to his companion, who stands on the other side of the frame or loom.

The best saddlebags are from Zacatecoluca. They are woven on a loom one end of which is fastened by a rope to the branch of a tree. The loom hangs down perpendicularly, the bottom weighted with stones or a heavy stick. The weaver sits on the ground on a stone or log, and firmly battens the fiber weft threads with a broad stick cut from hardwood. This process has a peculiar sound, so these looms have become known as *chillote* (noisy). In Chalatenango, *mezcalito* fiber is used to weave saddlebags. Two upright poles are planted in the ground at a required distance for the width of the saddlebags, and on these a man weaves. The saddlebags are finished off by doubling over the two ends and sewed at both sides with a large needle threaded with fiber. The middle or handle is braided in the weaving process, or the middle warp threads are allowed to remain loose without a weft crossing and later are firmly wound with colored fibers in separate units, to make a strong handle.

To prepare henequen, the following method is generally used: the leaves are cut and reduced to fiber by beating with a hard wooden club or mallet. The pulp is scraped away with a forklike utensil so as to leave only the fiber. This is well washed in river or lake, and hung out to dry. Once dry, it is combed repeatedly to separate the fibers, which are then tied into skeins. Two fibers or more are spun into string and later worked into rope. Both men and women use the *taravilla*, a small wooden instrument, one end of which is rap-

Apulo Beach, Lake Ilopango.

Lake Ilopango in the evening.

Old El Salvador. Indian ruins at San Andrés (above) and those at El Tazumal (below).

New El Salvador. Ilopango Airport (above) and the 5 de Noviembre Dam (below).

The Volcano of Izalco, by night and by day.

The old colonial church at Metapán.

The lakes and the rivers: Lake Atescatempa (above) and the Lempa
River (below).

The mountains and the valleys: Las Pavas (the Virgin's) Hill, seen from across the valley. Below is the Campo de Marte Park in San Salvador, with the mountains in the distance.

Statue of the Indian warrior Atonatl at Atecozol.

The Cathedral of Santa Ana.

idly twirled around an axle, while another operator feeds
to it the two-ply fiber strands. Rope is twisted on a large
wooden wheel turned rapidly by a handle, winding the
string into a two- or three-ply rope. Medium thick rope is
sold by *brazadas*: one dozen units each six yards long. Besides the above mentioned plants used for fiber, a very fine
string is made out of two-ply coconut fiber (Cocos nucifera).
The fiber of the banana plant (Musa) is used occasionally,
as also the above-mentioned fiber of the *Abaca* plant (Musa
textiles) or Manila hemp.

The most famous centers for this craft are regions where
fiber plants grow in abundance, such as San Miguel, Suchitoto, and Chirilagua.

MATS

This craft is one of the most skilled. For many years Salvadorean mats have been traded to neighboring countries.
Famed centers are well known, and perhaps the best are the
villages of Nahuizalco and San Pedro Perulapán.

In the first named village, rushes grow on the nearby hills
and rich bottom lands. They must be planted when the
moon is new. Even at the driest period of the year, these
bottom lands are always moist. The rushes attain about
seven feet and when full grown are cut by the Indians with
a large knife, known in this country as *corvo*. Four days are
required to dry the rushes in the sun. Three units are slit
lengthwise with a knifelike small implement of wood *(raja-
dores)*. Some of the units are colored, others are left in their
natural state. They are exposed to heavy dew for several
nights to make them soft and pliable. This much is the work
of the men. Then the women take over and weave the mats
by hand. The usual technique is to start at one corner of the
new mat and weave the strands over and under diagonally.
The colored strands are inserted at intervals, according to
the pattern design. The mats from this region are famous
because they are woven out of long and even strands. The
ends are deftly turned back and inserted underneath various
woven strands so that they are held firmly.

The mats from San Pedro Perulapán compete with the above in their wearing qualities. The ones woven in Santa Catarina Masahuat and Chirilagua are also of good quality.

Acapetates, a special kind of mat which serves many purposes, are woven from the *vara de cohete* and *vara de carrizo* (Arundo donax L., Poaceae), which are strong glossy reeds thicker than those used for other varieties of mats. These mats serve equally well as walls, coverings for stands, roofs, and not unfrequently take the place of capes and umbrellas.

Mats are woven from the rushes of the *tule Silvestre* (Cyperus canus, Presl. Ciperaceae), and other species of the genus Cyperus growing abundantly all over this country. A so-called tule, growing in the swamps near the village of Ateos (Typha angustifolia Fam. Tifaceae) must be included in the above list. In this warm climate every household needs a mat. From the highest to the lowest, mats are indispensable. A brisk trade is carried on at every market and fair, and the buyer instinctively recognizes the superior output from well-known villages.

Hats

The weaving of hats is a major craft, and the finest are made in Izalco. Two varieties are distinct: those woven of braided strands and those woven of plain palm leaf strands. Both are well made. The Izalco woven hats belong to the last named variety.

The young palm leaves are cut three days before the full moon, to insure their lasting quality. The strands are wet continually during the weaving process with cloths saturated in clean water. The work starts at the center of the crown: the greater the number of strands woven into a hat, the better the quality. The palm leaves must be well dried and cut in even strands; some are colored to achieve designs and a few are tinted with aniline dyes or colored black.

The finest hats are woven of the *palma de montaña* (forest palm), as well as from the *palma de corozo,* the *palmilla,* and other rushes, depending on the region wherein the craft is practiced. Hats are bleached and stiffened for commercial trade by the use of a solution of oxalic acid, sulphur, and starch. The true Indian hat is much more limp. The best known centers for hat weaving are San Antonio Masahuat, Sensuntepeque, San Pedro Puxtla, and Tenancingo.

BASKETS

This is a well-developed craft of superior quality. The best known and most typical basket is that used for market, very shallow and strong. The best kinds are the *Viroleños* of a peculiar brownish color woven in Zacatecoluca. Seldom, one might almost say never, does an Indian or lower-class *ladino* deign to carry a basket with a handle. Large or small baskets are balanced securely on the woman's head, supported by a *yagual* or circle of cloth to lessen the pressure on the head.

Perhaps the most useful baskets are the oblongs of all sizes, *tumbillas,* generally with a tightly fitted shallow lid. They serve equally well for a baby crib, valise, or any of numerous household requirements. Mostly wide and deep, with no decorations, they are woven of the *vara de carrizo,* the same reed used for the *acapetates. Tumbillas* without lids are a specialty of San Pedro Perulapán. The Nahuizalco Indians weave the best with lids.

Cestillos are woven in Cojutepeque from a vine resembling the morning-glory. Baskets woven with the *Caña de Castilla* are a specialty of villages in the department of Sonsonate. Apaneca is renowned for baskets woven of the fibers of the coconut palm, baskets which are very fine and artistic. The *palma de sombrero* (hat palm) is used in Tenancingo. Lianas of different varieties and plants belonging to the wicker family are also in demand for baskets in the innumerable villages that send their crafts to markets and fairs. Baskets made from the *mashaste* plant (Arrabidae Chica, Bignonaceae) are also much in demand. The Salvadorean shallow baskets with strands highly colored with aniline dyes are pretty, and have become a special trading feature of the fair held in connection with the pilgrimage to Esquipulas in Guatemala.

The technique of one and all is practically the same, with the splints of wicker, rush, or reed moistened until pliable, then crossed until they ray out from a central hub like the spokes of a wheel. Warp splints are woven in and out of the main splints. The finished article is always artistic, as are all the fast vanishing hand crafts.

CERAMICS

Two methods are employed for this craft: those exclusively prepared and molded by hand by women in the same manner as they were made in pre-Columbian days, and the product of the potter's wheel and kiln or earth ovens, made only by men. Many villages specialize in a great variety of shapes and are keen rivals for the reputation of their villages, where the craft is carried on by the first method. Various centers are recognized for typical specimens. Paleca craft is confined to large-sized jars (*cántaros*), cooking pots (*ollas*), and platelike flat dishes (*comales*). The method is of the simplest: the clay is mixed with river sand and water and left to settle for several days. It is then strained from one receptacle to another by means of a sieve made out of a gourd. When thoroughly cleaned, it is again allowed to settle, before spreading on the ground to dry. The woman molds the clay over an old dish with her wet hands. If an article is small, then no mold is used. When the clay is dry, the ground vessel is removed, and the finishing touches, such as handles and fluted opening, are skillfully added. The surface is repeatedly rubbed with a celt or smooth stone to give it a polished appearance. If the vessel is to be decorated, a fine red clay (*tahuite*) is dissolved in water and applied with a corn husk. This basic technique with slight variations is that generally used for the first method. The *comales* are shaped by taking a large lump of kneaded clay. The woman spreads it on the ground, manipulating it rapidly around and

around until the flat shape is molded, meanwhile patting it
into shape with a very wet cloth.

Primitive ceramics are fired by placing them on large
stones on the ground, and covering them with straw, dry
leaves, or twigs, whichever is handier. The fire burns for at
least two hours and is carefully watched. Many of the vessels
have artistic irregular black dots and dashes sprinkled over
the surface. This is achieved by dipping a corn husk into the
liquid or the mashed fruit of the *Capulín montés* or of
the *nance* and, while the article is still hot, it is sprinkled
with this concoction.

Clay articles are indispensable to every household, whether
Indian or *ladino*. The vessels are useful as well as decorative
for the kitchen. The best molded ceramics come from villages such as Panchimalco, Apopa, Ilobasco, and Paleca.

Ceramics molded on the potter's wheel are of a better
quality, with good glaze and polish, but are definitely a trade
article. Many workshops are dedicated to this kind of work,
and both the potter's wheel and earth ovens are used to supply the demand for these ceramics. Several are located in the
vicinity of San Salvador City. Quezaltepeque is well known
for its output of this ware, which eventually will crowd the
artistic hand molded ceramics into oblivion, for quality will
be neglected in favor of quantity.

GOURDS

The first bowls, dippers, jugs, and cups were fashioned
from gourds. Primitive tribes found the fruit of the *Morro*
tree useful. From the Cucurbitacea vines they also obtained
gourds, which we call calabashes. As gourds became known,
thriving centers developed in the regions where the *Morro*
tree and the vines flourished.

The round fruit of the *Morro* tree was converted into
guacales, and the oblong variety into *jícaras.* Both these articles are indispensable to an Indian household. The dried
fruits without any decoration, either *guacales* or *jícaras,*
meaning bowls or cups, are known as *cheles.* For these the

fruit is cut in halves or quarters, the pulp and seed are cleaned out, then the hard shell is well boiled in a heavy solution of limewater and dried in the sun. The result is a clean utensil, attained at a minimum cost, and discarded when its usefulness is over.

For the decorated gourds, the procedure is as follows: The fruit is cut in half, cleaned, and the shell is rubbed with the leaves of the *Guarumo* tree. The black color is given with the *tinaco*: fermented corn, water, and oxidized nails placed in one receptacle, and in another the *Nacascolo* fruit boiled in water. The gourd is dipped first into one solution and dried in the sun, then into the second, and again dried. This is done repeatedly until the desired shade of black is obtained. For a good polish, powdered charcoal is mixed with lemon juice. The surface is rubbed and the gourd exposed to the sun repeatedly. Then the craftsmen decorate the gourd with any sharp instrument that is handy, an umbrella rib serving admirably. The design, either etched or cut into the black surface in high or low relief, stands out handsomely against the dark background.

Of great interest and probably the only place in Central America where this technique is still extant is the village of Izalco. After the gourd has been cleaned, dried, and processed and the design drawn on the surface, then grease is applied carefully to the design. Left to cool, the article is dyed black by the afore-mentioned process, or stained with a mixture of grease and lampblack secured from the smoke of the pitch pine. Once dried, it is held over a fire and a cloth dipped in very hot water cleans away the melted grease covering the design. This leaves the design white and clear against the black background of the gourd. This technique is scientifically known as "negative," and ceramics from the earliest pre-Columbian era are decorated in this way.

Izalco is also famous for the first named variety of gourds. Other villages make only the undecorated utensils. The fruit of the calabash vine is much used for receptacles, but these are never as artistic as those made from the fruit of the *Morro* tree. A very large Cucurbitaceae fruit called *tol* or *taro* is used for household articles, either painted or plain. When decorated in very bright colors, they are tourist trade pieces, mostly in imitation of trade pieces from Mexico. The fruit of this vine grows to such large proportions that halves are cleaned and dried to serve admirably as basins in which to bathe small children.

Minor Crafts

The Indians or lower-class *ladinos* carry on lesser crafts besides the major crafts just mentioned. These minor crafts are distinctly Salvadorean.

Corn Husk Dolls—From the tiniest one-inch doll to large ones about ten inches high, these figures are beautifully made from dried corn husks. Every item is correctly depicted and the costumes are those worn in different parts of the country by Indians and *ladinos*. Formerly, however, these dolls were symbols of corn fertility.

Chinta Dolls—These are wooden dolls carved out of one piece of hardwood and cleverly painted with a few dabs of color. They are the precious possessions of young children, and, of course, quite impossible to clothe.

Ilobasco Clay Figures and Dishes—These are the feature of sales on the streets of San Salvador during the weeks preceeding and following Christmas. Tiny dishes and figures are exquisitely molded by hand, or by wood molds. The hereditary artists who carry on this work have preserved this art, using the clay deposits near the town of Ilobasco. The clay is manipulated, kneaded, and mixed with the resinous extract of the *escobillo* plant to make it stick in the desired shape. The articles are baked in earth ovens or kilns of the more primitive style, then painted in vivid colors.

The specialties of these artists are the figures of the Holy Family and the manger at Bethlehem. It is almost incredible the way that the tiniest figures come to life under the artist's hand. Most of the output is used by the city people to make their *portales* or *nacimientos,* which are typical of Christmas and take the place of a Christmas tree. Some of the figures are exported to neighboring countries.

The best room of the house is dedicated to the *nacimiento.* This occupies the entire floor and mountains and rivers, villages and towns are laid out in detail—farms with cattle and poultry, trails along mountain roads, with Indians and *ladinos* scattered along a scene that is simulated in miniature. The pièce de résistance is the crêche, cave, or shelter where the Holy Night scene of the Nativity is staged, either with large or small figures, complete to the animals and fowls mentioned in the Scriptures. When the owner can afford it, mechanical toys are added to amuse the audience: a tiny railroad impelled by electricity, or a roaring stream of water, which cascades down the mountainside from a hidden faucet into an equally hidden outlet. It was formerly the custom, rarely observed nowadays, that every visitor to view the *nacimiento* received some refreshment. A *nacimiento* cannot be described; it must be seen to appreciate the uncountable things that are gathered for its conception and arranged so realistically.

Wooden Stirrups—There are many kinds of wooden stirrups, but the most noteworthy are those having carved tops with a double-headed eagle, the symbol of Charles V, the specialty of the village of Opico.

Powder Puffs—Not an Indian craft, but definitely typical of this country, powder puffs are made from goose feathers. They are shaped to fit into ladies' pocketbooks, and are great items of commerce in neighboring countries. The puffs are a specialty of Ahuachapán.

Silk Shawls (Chalinas)—Exquisitely colored in pastel shades with long complicated knotted fringes, these shawls are woven on early foot looms, and are a recognized specialty. The silk is the Chinese untwisted silk, which is scarce

at the present time so that these exquisite shawls are seldom
seen now.

Leather Craft—Sundry articles both utilitarian and luxury
—well-finished bags, sandals, purses, and sheaths for knives—
find a ready market.

TRADE ROUTES

El Salvador is crisscrossed by trails which are in reality
re-established trade routes of long ago. The people inherited from their Indian forefathers the instinct for trading.
Nowadays, trading is largely restricted within the country,
because of customs tariff barriers of other countries, with
the exception of a steady flow of the lesser crafts to the fair
at Esquipulas, a pilgrimage for the week before January
15, and to some of the fairs in Honduras. It is amazing how
far specialties from certain regions are sent to different fairs
and markets in the country.

The trade instinct of the Salvadorean people is renowned
in the rest of Central America. For example, in Costa Rica
certain woolen materials for men's garments were attributed
to Salvador, when in reality it was Guatemalan highland
wool material, but traded farther south by people from this
country. Also famous, even to the north of the South American continent, were the Salvadorean afore-mentioned silk
shawls.

No fair or large market is complete without traders selling saddlebags woven in Cacaopera, hammocks and rope
from Chalatenango, Azacualpa, and Cuyotitlán. If the need
is for a saddle with the top section lined in leather, then the
trader from Cojutepeque is awaited with his merchandise.
Large hampers, *tumpillas,* from Zacatecoluca, Olocuintla,
San Pedro Perulapán, and Nahuizalco are trade specialties, and also palm leaf hats woven in Tenancingo, Masagua,
Chilanga, and Izalco. When a special kind of mat is desired,
then the trader from Nahuizalco is looked for, sitting side by
side in a shady nook under the *Amatle* tree with the man

displaying his ceramics from Quezaltepeque, or the woman
with her wares from Paleca. Food and flavoring ingredients
from far-off regions are traded: *Chacalines* [1] (shrimp) from
the Pacific Coast, or the peppers of different kinds.

Special herbs and medicinal plants whose roots and leaves,
flowers and fruit are even now the pharmacopoeia of the
lower classes (see page 125) occupy a special corner where
these remedies, vegetable, animal, and mineral are spread
on a clean mat, some from nearby regions, others from far-
flung places difficult to reach.

The above-mentioned trade specialties are the best known,
but there are dozens of others that are also carried over trails
and roads from one end of the country to the other.

[1] The word *Chacalin* is used in the Republic of Costa Rica to mean a
young child.

XII

DANCES

Dances and Costumes

IN ALMOST all the small villages, *bailes* or *areytos* take place during the celebration of religious festivities and fairs. Some are hardly worth mentioning, while others are spectacularly carried out in more or less indigenous forms. Dancing during religious festivities and great occasions has been one of the traditions (*costumbres*) of the Indians; in ancient days some were dedicated to special deities invoking their good will when going to war. Others were typical of the time for planting or harvesting the crops; a great many symbolized fertility rites. But dancing for the pure joy of rhythm, like the present-day form, with non-Indian people, was never an Indian custom. Nor is it at the present time, excepting in villages where a good deal of *ladino* influence has mingled with the Indian.

During the colonial period, many of the dances were suppressed by the priests, who saw in them with justified reason idolatrous disguise. Nevertheless, more than one of the ancient dances survives under a very thin veneer of later interpretation.

For most of the dances, great preparations must be made before the day they are to be staged. For weeks, and even months, men must learn the steps and give long hours to rehearsals of the words. Formerly the words were taught by rote and most of them still are, though occasionally a headman of the village will have a written manuscript of the words, which were written down during the colonial era. It is a privilege or a penance to take part in the dance. The actors must provide their own costumes, a part of which is a cloth which swaths the head and that part of the face not covered by the mask. This cloth must not be removed during the several days and nights of the celebration. This is done in compliance with a *promesa* (*vow*), which the individual has made to God or perhaps to a special deity, so as to achieve celestial recompense, or absolution for a penance he has imposed on himself. Women are not allowed to participate in the more primitive dances, and their place is taken by men, who dress in women's costumes.

The costumes depend upon the dance, ranging from skins of animals to very elaborate colonial regalia, and some queer and quite unrelated modern adaptations, such as umbrellas, high boots, top hats, and so forth. Cotton in gay colors is the material chosen for the costumes, with lace, ribbons, tinsel, and every imaginable gaudy bauble. The dress tries to portray what the character is supposed to be, as the words are mostly unintelligible through the thick mask and surrounding textile. The masks are distinctive: of cloth, coconut fiber, wood, or gourd; blue masks and red masks, the first supposedly representing the Moors, and the latter the Christians in some of the dances imported by the conquerors. Why this particular distinction, I cannot say. Other masks have zoomorphic figures on the head; others have rings with beads, especially green ones, between the lips. The variety is endless, and each one more ugly than the last.

Golden locks of henequen fiber simulating hair hang to the shoulders of the personages portraying the conquerors, kings, and princes of the sixteenth and seventeenth centuries. Flowers, shells, bits of tin and glass all add to the general effect. Spanish weapons of days long gone by such as the *Partesana* sword, are added. Calico Mother Hubbards, straw hats with paper flowers, bright colored hose, are indispensable items.

The best known dances are *La Historia, El Tunco de Monte,* and *Los Tronos,* popular in the western part of the country. In the eastern section, probably the best known are *La Partesana* and different versions of *La Historia,* such as

Fernando VII and *Charlemagne,* though each village and each hamlet has its individual version of some dance that has been preserved through the centuries.

La Historia is a dance pageant depicting battles of the religious wars during the Middle Ages between Christians and Moors, the struggle between the Cross and the Crescent, and has absolutely no relation to the background of these Indians or to episodes of the Spanish Conquest. The steps are not complicated and the music is provided by a *chirimia* and drum, with shrill sounds announcing the appearance of groups of dancers with their entourage during the August feasts in the Capital.[1]

The costumes for the above dance are the most spectacular of all. The actors are divided into Christians and Moors, the steps are dignified and carried out with many gestures of the hands. The underlying tenor is deeply religious, and in most of the versions of this dance it is dedicated to the Virgin Mary, and ends, of course, with the Christians achieving a definite triumph over the Moors.

In some of these dances, an individual represents a jester (*gracejo*), dressed in tatters of queer odds and ends, or he may represent an animal of the lowest order, such as a rat. This individual cavorts around the dancers, raising his voice above the monotonous tones of the dancers' speeches. Long perorations of very lewd character are his specialty, to the great delight of the spectators. In the villages of San Antonio Abad, Cuzcatlancingo, and neighboring hamlets, this character is the most prominent among the dancers.

In Paleca, the dance of San Sebastian is staged with a colorful and worthwhile setting. The masks have large and weird zoomorphic figures, representing the Nahual or familiar spirit, which was supposed to be the companion of the Indian during his lifetime, dying when he died: the human part of this duality, when in dire stress, was able to

---

[1] *La Fiesta de la Cruz,* which takes place in many villages on May 3, is well staged: the houses have altars loaded with fruit. The belief is that if not celebrated fittingly, the Devil enters and remains in the house during the year.

convert himself at will into his companion animal form to protect himself. The costumes for this dance are in bright colors, and the saint is decked out with bits of lace curtains and ribbons to add to the general effect of gaudiness.

The *Tunco del Monto (Cujtan-Cuyamet)* is a dance of the mountain pig, which has a decided pre-Columbian flavor. The chief character is covered by a large pigskin. When the pig he represents is killed at some village corner after many hours of monotonous recitals, the entire procession and populace stop, and the pieces figuratively cut from the pig are handed around to the bystanders by the man who has killed the pig; this individual is dressed in a Spanish costume of the sixteenth century. He is adept in repartee, and as he hands around the meat he is supposed to cut from his victim, he utters lewd remarks and doubtful jokes about village characters to the glee of the multitude. Intermingled in the monologue are pleas to the deities for propitious weather for abundant crops. It is typically Indian, as surely the sacrifice of a pig should pacify the deities and assure the village a prosperous year.[1]

The dance *Jeu Jeu,* which takes place in Izalco, makes a good deal of noise and is a prolonged festival. Twelve men dance around in a circle, wherein stands the headman. They are all dressed to represent savage men, *Jicaques,* with grasses and palm leaves, gilt crowns with large feathers, bracelets and leg ornaments adorning their bare bodies. The dance rhythm tinkles the shells and waves the plumes. Every so often the shrill cries of *Jeu Jeu* fill the air. After many turns, the twelve men kneel around the chief and again shrilly cry *Jeu Jeu* (let the rains come, let the rains come), and the sound echoes back from the distant hills: "this will be done, this will be done." The wild men flourish on high their bows and arrows, and in a wild whirl of music and sounds the dance ends. Now the *cofradias* each take their

---

[1] *Las Pulgas* is a dance performed in Santiago Texaguangos. A man represents a flea, another a louse, and two old and ugly women take the part of coy young maidens. On the whole it is long, unintelligent, and without rhyme or reason.

turn, and with the same wild cry typifying their racial unity (*Jeu Jeu*) they bring their special saints to take part in these festivities. The members of the principal *cofradia*, El Padre Eterno, look impressive, when they appear bearing poles of bare wood, the branches decorated with corncobs of different colors to represent the directions of Heaven: red—east, white—north, yellow—south, black—west, each color and stick decorated with seven corncobs. No women are allowed to touch these poles, otherwise bad crops will be the result. While these poles are kept in the *cofredia* house, they are considered a sacred emblem and charge.

La Barreña is a dance of the *Mengalas* that is no longer performed, but the music is still played. It used to be danced by couples, the man with a black cloth in his hand and the woman with a large handkerchief.[1] Other typical dances at the present time are: *El Panadero, La Sebastiana, El Negrito, La Shora, El Venadito,* and *La Partesana.* The first named have a decided post-Conquest flavor; the last named are much more of pre-Columbian survival, as is the typical *Jeu-Jeu* dance, wherein the thirteen months of the ancient pre-Columbian calendar are mentioned. Each individual used to recite or sing to his special month and place in this calendar a formal supplication to the deities that provide benefits to humanity. This feature ended with the savage cry, *Jeu Jeu* (without any meaning), but typical of this people.[2]

INDIAN MUSIC

As with everything else, most of the Indian music is basically connected with that of the Mexican Indians, and developed in this country along well-defined lines, according to the Indians' environment. The three periods of the history are also well marked in the Indian music of the present day: the one which preserves a true indigenous influence;

[1] Two well-known centers provide dance costumes. The largest is in a suburb of Santiago San Salvador; the other is in San Antonio Abad.

[2] *El Torito Pinto* is a dance of post-Columbian flavor, wherein five men fight a bull that chases the men to the amusement of the spectators.

the second, a mixture of Indian music with that of colonial importation, resulting in the very typical music of this country; and later-day music that preserves Indian elements mixed with colonial and other foreign elements, including, in the last decade, a few bars of jazz and other tunes, not at all in accordance with the basic style of the Indian music.

The first songs of a primitive people were those of a religious nature, or the expression of exuberant joy or grief. The Indians had to express vocally with extemporaneous tunes their wish to adore Nature when at its best, or to pacify the elements at their worst. The temples where sacrificial rites took place brought forth from the awe-struck multitude songs of deep-rooted hatred toward their enemies.

They sang different songs for each season: songs with cadences through which run a fine thread of lament when the cold winds arrive to announce the harvest season and the end of summer; a mournful song, a wail of protest against the elements of the rainy season. Songs that are gay and lilting, when the warm sun awakes the Indian with promises of plenty; deep-toned songs to the sun, to the moon, and the deities. The song asking for the first rains to fructify the grain is the song that the Indian sings out of the joy of his soul, when he contemplates the trees bursting into bud, and the fields taking on the first lush green tinge of the new crops.

However, Indian music is seldom truly gay; a melancholy pervades the whole in character with the Indian's nature. It leans to fanaticism and a more warlike and emphatic expression in all its tones than those of the softer and more rhythmical Maya music. The most potent influence of the Indian music was inspired by Nature in all its manifestations: the songs of birds, the wind in the trees, the waves of the sea as they reached the shore, the rain, the sound of water as it rushes down the streams or waterfalls.

The primitive form of the music was based on the pentatonic tonal scale, or a similar five-toned scale. The pentatonic scale of five whole tones and the five-toned scale in turn were composed of five different notes or sounds, though having a half tone. Therefore, the early music never went beyond a "fifth" note. The first instruments sounded only simple monotones. Instruments whereon musical scales could be achieved made their appearance later on.

Clay whistles, reeds, and hollow twigs were employed for the rare polytonal musical instruments. Of the first named, there were also bitonal and tritonal instruments. The Indians knew and used percussion, string, and wind instruments, as well as those having vibrating membranes or thongs to produce the different sounds.

During the colonial period, the Indian pentatonic tonal scale acquired a sixth note, or colonial note, and later, as further influences mixed with it, the scale reached seven notes, the diatonic scale of modern musical methods.

Instruments—Of the pre-Columbian type of instruments, at the present time only the following survive: the *huehuetl*, which is considered the most primitive, consisting of a cylinder of clay in different shapes or of wood, having on the top side a cover of deerskin tightly drawn; it is played with the hands, fingers, or a stick with a large rubber head and has three kinds of legs to stand it on end. The *teponahaustle* is a hollow cylindrical piece of wood with thick walls, usually a tree trunk, placed horizontally on the ground. In the middle upper surface it has a rectangular opening with two different tongues cut out of the log, which produce the sounds when played. The sticks with which this instrument is played have rubber heads and produce an intensely loud sound in two distinct tones at intervals of a third. These tones can travel for long distances.

The "drum" is made of a section of hollowed wood with its ends covered with parchment. The different sizes are known as *atabal (kettle drum)*, *tamborcito (small drum)*. Other instruments are: the *sacabuche* or *sambumbia*, the *caramba*, also called *guarambamba* or *Chistatle*, and the *tortuga* or *ayotl*. The latter is an empty turtle shell played with two sticks and producing sounds similar to those of the small drum. The *ayacachtli* and the *caramba* are percussion instruments. *Quijadas* or *tarasca* (jawbones of animals) are clicked together rhythmically to produce musical sounds.

The reed fife or *pito de caña* and *chirimia* are typical in all village festivities. The performer's ability to produce harmonious sounds is marvelous, especially on the cane flute, which has six holes in the reed tube and three scales progressing from C to B with corresponding naturals and flats obtained by blowing into the reed with greater or lesser force. The semitones are obtained by partially closing the tonal holes.

To the above-mentioned flute and *chirimia* must be added the instruments producing melodious tones, like the *flautilla de los sacrificios,* now used only in the more primitive villages during the processions of Holy Week, particularly the one on Good Friday. I have mentioned some of the different varieties of flutes that are still in use and are reminiscent of ancient pagan rites. The smaller and narrower instruments give forth a painful and shrill sound; the broader and longer ones have a much fuller and more melodious sound resembling the modern flute.

The *caramba, guarambamba,* or *chistatle* is a percussion instrument very typical of this country and not found elsewhere in Central America. It is shaped like a bow and arrow with a taut wire string, having in the middle of the shaft a hollow gourd open at one side. This instrument is played by partially closing the opening of the gourd while the string is tapped with a small stick to produce the vibrations. The notes, both in tone and intensity, are at best very imperfect, but an experienced player brings forth a semblance of musical tones that are rather sweet and stirring.

During the Colonial period the Indians adopted guitars, trumpets, and other European instruments, and combined them with their own instruments to produce their forefathers' music. The *marimba,* perhaps the best known of the instruments, has been a subject of controversy. Whether, as some maintain, it is an imported instrument, or whether it is truly pre-Columbian, is not the question. It was known long before the Conquest as an instrument that hung from the neck of the musician, with a keyboard of long gourds, over which hardwood plates or keys were placed in sizes calculated to give the notes of the scale when sounded with two sticks tipped with rubber. This *marimba* had a keyboard of natural tones, and the semitones were obtained by placing a piece of wax on the key before striking it. In villages in Western El Salvador, a very primitive small *marimba* may still be heard. It has only three octaves and is played by one performer, who hangs it around his neck in the same way as the original instrument was hung.

Later the *marimba* was converted into a modern instrument, and after many experiments a second keyboard with semitones was added and the gourd sounding board was replaced by wooden boxes. The best wood was found to be that of the *hormiga* or *hormiguillo* tree, which must be seasoned for at least six months by hanging it where the sun and chimney smoke might impregnate it. Nowadays this instrument is seldom heard by itself, except in far-off villages; to the modern substitute a whole gamut of other instruments known to the musical world has been added. Not the least noisy is a hollow gourd filled with pebbles and with a stick inserted for a handle, which the player violently swings up and down and around, so that the sound of the *chinchines* may be heard above the din of the other instruments.

Musicians and singers were highly thought of by the community. They supposedly were the ones who preserved the traditions of the past by their music and their songs.

It must be added that the musical instruments were not always favorably looked upon after the Conquest. A Royal Decree of July 29, 1565, ordered that all instruments and singers must be strictly organized in the monasteries by the chief of the religious orders. Since musical instruments were kept in the monasteries, the chief would be able to restrain their use, particularly by young boys who were interned there, and thus prevent their addiction to music and the possibility of their becoming laggards with unmentionable vices.

The so-called *loas* are songs of Spanish origin. Two individuals are placed on opposite sides: the Devil and the Angel. The chant is in honor of the Patron Saint of the village and usually takes place in front of the principal citizen's house where an altar has been erected in the street so that the procession may stop and a priest may give a benediction. Though very post-colonial, it is carried out by all lower-class individuals.

Thanks to Doña María M. de Baratta for her technical assistance with Indian music, which is her specialty.

XIII

THE ARTS

THE artistic influences of the pre-Columbian Indian were derived from so many sources that one cannot say definitely that this or that one influences the present-day artistic movements. The colonial friars brought out to America European artistic movements of various periods, but because of the many disasters through which this country has passed very few can be said to have survived in any distinct form, or greatly to have influenced modern artists.

The poverty, political and terrestrial upheavals, and the greater attraction of the capital of the kingdom for the artists led to a notable decadence in art in the colonial era among the Indians. The convents and churches had a few noteworthy sculptures and paintings, but these have now disappeared.

This explains why the present-day art movement in El Salvador is complete in itself, with scant relationship to the past pre-Columbian and colonial backgrounds. Artists are developing on their own initiative, inspired by the rugged landscape, perpetual blue skies, and sunshine to transmit to their canvases or to their books something innately Salvadorean, which cannot be compared with or said to be derived from any outside influences.

LITERATURE

In the modern field the outstanding figure is Francisco Gavidia, who at one time or another has translated into Spanish famous songs from operas, from the English, French, and German, in addition to well-known poetry in these languages. He has written a score of books on archaeological, regional, and deeply scientific subjects, and also on the theater. He was the co-founder with Francisco Galindo of the National Theater *(Teatro Nacional)*.

Interesting Indian legends have been preserved by Joaquín Aragón and a score of other good writers who have produced really worthwhile literature in the modern era.

It is well to mention that just after the independence a Salvadorean, Francisco Cisneros (1823-1878), won fame in Cuba, and was the first colonial to direct the Academy of San Alejandro de Habana. Part of his work is now in the National Museum of Havana.

During the colonial period, Juan José Bernal, a priest, wrote delightful poetry. A few of the modern writers were influenced by the poetry of the Nicaraguan poet, Rubén Darío. Alberto Masferrer was considered an international writer, foremost as a speaker and a prolific writer of modern sociological trend. No less famous in the field of letters are several others at the present time, such as Maria de Baratta, Claudia Lars (Carmen Branon de Samayoa Chinchilla) famous poetess, Serafin Quiteño, a poet, Quino Caso, Ricardo Martel Caminos, Luis Gallegos Valdés, Napoleón Viera Altamirano, and Ricardo Trigueros de León.

José Batres Móntúfar, an internationally recognized poet and writer, was born in El Salvador on March 18, 1809; in reality he belongs to the writers of Guatemala, where he went to live in 1822, and where he was buried when he died in 1844.

The list of modern writers is long and each of them is endeavoring to produce literature that will take its place with that of the continental writers.

PAINTING

The outstanding painter is Salazar Arrué, known as Salarrué. He is famous for his tapestries, in which he portrays the exuberant Salvadorean vegetation and figures belonging to the soil. He is also well known as an author. Alberto Guerra

Trigueros is an author and painter. José Mejía Vides does woodcuts and paintings of Indian and *ladino* figures that always attract a crowd wherever they are exhibited as also do the works of the artists Julia Diaz, Angel Salinas, Elas Reyes, and Pedro de Montúfar.

These are just a few of the artists I might mention who are depicting the ever-changing landscape and the attractive Salvadorean panorama.

MUSIC AND THEATER

Modern music distinctly Salvadorean has one representative whose endeavor is toward preserving the Indian music, Maria de Baratta. Several violinists and other instrumentalists are outstanding. The *Sociedad Protectora de la Sinfónica Salvadoreña* is composed of music lovers in the capital, to protect and encourage the Symphonic Orchestra and bring to El Salvador outstanding artists from all over the world. Alezandro Cuidad Real is a fine musician, a member of the *Sinfonica;* Angela Garcia Peña "la Sol" (Graciela Huezo Paredes) is also a first-rate musician.

In this country there has been an interest in the study of recitation and several individuals have achieved success in the field.

Theater—In this field there has been great endeavor and at one time or another the *Escuala de Prácticas Escénicas* has helped further to develop talent for the stage.

La Banda Militar (The Military Band)—At the present time it is one of the best in America; it plays regularly in the different parks to large audiences who take advantage of the cool afternoon and evening hours to listen to good musical programs.

An amusing incident deals with the origin of this band. At the beginning of 1841, there arrived in the town of San Miguel from the island of Cuba three musicians well versed in the playing of band instruments. Colonel D. Manuel

Cañas, the military commander of the town, heard them and was so entranced with their music that he conceived the idea of contracting with them in the name of the government to establish a military band in the capital. Señor Cañas and the townspeople regaled the musicians with all sorts of attentions, and asked them to provide the music for Holy Week before they proceeded to the capital.

A Costa Rican who was in San Miguel was enthusiastic over the music of the Cubans. He immediately started negotiations for these men to proceed with him to Costa Rica, and one night the four of them silently made their exit and slipped away. In the morning the commander was disagreeably surprised at their disappearance and started his mounted troops in pursuit of the fugitives. They had walked nine leagues and were surprised to find themselves halted and returned to San Miguel, and thence to the capital, where President General Malespín signed the contract and thereby created a military band of El Salvador.

This résumé attempts to give a very general picture of the arts; the list of artists in each sphere is long, and they are recognized as outstanding by artistic circles in the rest of the world.

XIV

ECONOMIC OUTLOOK

S LOWLY the country is becoming self-sustaining. About three quarters of the population form a low-income group with a limited buying power, but provide the manpower to develop agriculture and industries. The higher income groups control the finances of the country and are the main supporters of foreign trade, both import and export. Besides the famous agricultural exports, live stock, hides, and some manufactured goods are exported.

BANKING AND FINANCE

All commercial banking is concentrated in the *Banco Central de Reserva de El Salvador* (Central Bank). Among other flourishing banking institutions are the Bank of London and South America, *Banco Salvadoreño* (which has a superb building), *Banco Hipotecario de El Salvador, Banco Occidental, Banco de Comercio, Banco Agricola Comercial,* and *Banco de Credito Rural.*

The money unit is the *colón,* equivalent to 40 cents in U.S. money, and divided into 100 cents.

In 1934 the bylaws of the *Banco Central de Reserva de El Salvador* were formulated and the exchange was stabilized at between 2.49 and 2.51 for a dollar. This bank is the only one authorized to issue paper money. Twenty percent of the deposits in all the banks must be in national money, of which at least half must be deposited in the Central Bank, which has a controlling interest in the other national banks. As this bank does not take care of mortgages, *El Banco Hipotecario de El Salvador* was established as a semiofficial agent.

Gold currency may not be exported or taken out of the country by anyone. In 1943 the Executive power decreed that an organ of *La Sociedad Anónima* called *Mejoramiento Social* should be formed, consisting of three groups of shareholders: *El Banco Hipotecario, Federación de Cajas Rurales,* and private individuals.

A protégé of the *Banco Hipotecario* is the *Federación de Cajas de Crédito,* established in San Salvador by a group of prominent individuals on February 10, 1943. The object was to establish the *Cooperative de Cajas de Crédito Rurales Limitada.*

Each of the *Cajas Rurales* must have at least ten well-known members of good standing; the central organization has the duty of constant inspection and watches over the activities of these branches. From this beginning the *Cooperatives Rurales* have spread and grown and now comprise innumerable activities, such as small spinning enterprises, small coffee landowners, groups of handicraftsmen, such as makers of ceramics and hats, weavers of mats and baskets and makers of products of other primitive crafts which the owners now advantageously sell within the country or send to the Central Office in San Salvador; a store is annexed to this office for the display of the various articles, which are sold at retail or, upon order, in wholesale quantities.

The *Banco Hipotecario* watches over all these transactions, and from time to time by proper documentation and careful administration supplies the capital needed for the various organizations of the *Cajas de Crédito* and *Cajas de Crédito Rurales.*

A most interesting financial transaction was carried out on December 14, 1949, between the International Bank for Reconstruction and Development and the government of El Salvador, approving a loan of $12,545,000 (U.S. dollars) in favor of an Executive Commission for the Hydroelectric Development of the Lempa River in the Republic of El Salvador. This was to help in the financing of a project in charge of the commission for development of electric power sites on the Lempa River. El Salvador is a member in good standing of the above-mentioned bank.

This commission provides El Salvador with the needed electric power by using the waters of the Lempa River for generating the electricity for all branches of economic and social development, thereby providing a better living standard.

The project is located at Chorrera del Guayabo, fifty-eight kilometers to the northeast of San Salvador on the boundary between the departments of Chalatenango and Cabañas. The dam is approximately sixty-four meters high by some five hundred meters long, and is made of concrete. Two transmission lines will branch out from here: one toward San Miguel, the other to San Salvador. There is provision for further extension. Electricity in greater volume is at present urgently needed in agriculture, mining, and industry, and for domestic and municipal use.

The Harza Engineering Company of Chicago was consulted, made the studies of the Lempa River, and continues to be consulted as the work progresses. A good road to transport materials and equipment to the site of the dam has been constructed by the Salvadorean government, twenty-nine kilometers from Ilobasco to the site.

The loan is for twenty-five years at $4\frac{1}{4}$ percent interest and guaranteed by the Salvadorean government. Bonds for approximately thirteen million *colones* have been sold by the commission and will bring 5 percent interest; bonds of one hundred, five hundred, and a thousand *colones* have been eagerly bought.

This enterprise is of enormous significance, not only for El Salvador, for by its example it stimulates the other sister republics to renewed energy in initiating modern projects.

HISTORICAL DATA

The conquerors brought from Spain the *doblón, castellano, ducado, dobla,* and *escudo,* worth respectively 750,500,

365, 350 and 4.8 *maravedis,* a gold coin equivalent to four *duros.*

In 1537, the Mexican mint coined money for these countries, and Peruvian money also circulated. In 1733, Guatemala coined money for circulation in the kingdom. The first coins or *macacos,* pieces of eight, were minted in Honduras, and circulated freely until late in the nineteenth century.

During the colonial era, the system of monetary values was based on the *real* as its unit:

Coin	Reales	Dollars
Ocho escudos	16	$2.00
Doubloon	8	1.00
Peso	8	1.00
Toston	4	.50
Peseta	2	.25
Real		.125
Medio real	½	.0625
Cuartillo	¼	.0316

The first money coined in Guatemala was the *doubloon.* The *peseta columnaria* was coined in these countries, and called by this name because it had the royal coat of arms of Spain between two columns. Fifteen of these silver coins or *pesetas* weighed five grams.

After the independence, Guatemala continued to coin the currency for El Salvador, and specific money called *Prado y Cornejo* circulated from 1828 to 1832. During the period of federation of the United Provinces of Central America, federal money circulated throughout all these countries, and gold coins were restamped with the federal coat of arms.

Subsequently several attempts were made to coin money in El Salvador. Permission was granted to the *Sindicat General des Monadies de Paris* to start a mint in El Salvador in 1891. This privilege was transferred to the Central American Mint, Ltd., which erected buildings on the site now occupied by the National Printing Shop *(Imprenta Nacional)* in San Salvador.

The unit was established by a decree of October 1, 1892, a *colón* weighing twenty-five grams of silver, 0.900 fine, or 0.782 of an ounce troy. In 1892, a gold standard was decreed, based on a unit with a value of 1,612.953 grams for every *colón*. The last reform of the currency was effected in 1919 by which the *colón* was fixed as the monetary silver unit, the gold standard having proved a failure.

At the present time gold coin is not allowed to be exported. No money is coined in El Salvador at the present time. The silver and other small currencies in circulation are imported from the U.S.A. Because of the shortage of small change, a large importation of 10-cent pieces of United States money was effected during 1943, and has circulated in the country in place of the 25-cent piece or *colón*.

WEIGHTS AND MEASURES

The metrical system was adopted by a decree of August 26, 1885. The Salvadorean *vara,* according to a previous law, equals 836 millimeters. This *vara* is substituted for the yard in most of the sales of yard goods, and care must be taken not to mistake a *vara* for a yard. A *libra* (pound) equals 460 grams.

Length

1 meter (m.)	39.37 in.
1 kilometer (km, 1,000 m.)	0.62 mi.
1 foot	0.30 m.
1 yard	0.91 m.
1 mile	1.61 km.

Area

1 sq. m.	10.76 sq. ft.
1 sq. km.	0.39 sq. mi.
1 hectare (10,000 sq. m.)	2.47 acres

Volume

1 liter	1.06 qt.
1 hectoliter (100 liters)	2.84 bu.

Spanish Units

1 arroba	25 lbs.
1 quintal	101 lbs.
1 vara	33 in.
1 legua (league)	3 mi.

XV

AGRICULTURE AND INDUSTRY

CULTIVATED CROPS

EL SALVADOR is the wealthiest country in Central America because of its intensive agricultural development. First and foremost, agriculture is a deciding factor in the way of life of its inhabitants. The vast population helps to provide the manpower necessary for the crops. All regions of the country are intensely cultivated and, unlike conditions in some of the other republics, the large landholders are primarily people of this country. Except for the few Indians and small landholders, agriculture is carried out with the most modern machinery and implements.

Coffee—The principal crop at the present time is coffee. It is said that Salvadorean coffee ranks high on the markets of the world, because of its splendid flavor. The first coffee tree was planted by a Brazilian schoolmaster, Antonio J. Coelho, in 1840. Coffee was first exported to the United States in 1881. The 1954-55 export figures (to October 31, 1955) show a total of 1,052,342 bags of 69 kilos (152 lbs.) each.

The principal centers for coffee production are the zones around San Salvador, Santa Ana, Santa Tecla, San Miguel, Santiago de María, and Sonsonate. Large shade trees have to be planted to protect the coffee trees. The leguminous *Pepeto* tree, which closes its leaves at night—thus permitting the dew to pass through to the coffee trees—and opens its leaves at sunrise to prevent evaporation is a popular tree. On other plantations the *Madre Cacao* tree is used, while other trees have from time to time been tried with a view to bettering the coffee production, as also has growing coffee without shade. The coffee season starts in November and lasts about three months. It is a busy time for the owners and workers on coffee plantations.

The ripe coffee berries are picked by hand into large baskets. In very steep places the pickers are strapped to the trees while they garner the fruit. A migrant group of workmen and their families assemble from distant villages to gather the crops. Despite the primitive and slow handwork of harvesting the coffee, it is cleaned and prepared for export in the most modern mills with up-to-date equipment.

Sugar—This crop is grown in many places, but principally in the departments of San Salvador, La Libertad, and Sonsonate. However, there are many small mills worked by animal power that produce the brown *panela* and sugar loaf, both popular among the general public. Sugar refineries are equipped with modern machinery and the quality of this product is high.

Honey—It is exported in greater or less quantities. Because of the many wild flowers the bees produce a delicately flavored honey that is much in demand.

Henequen—This crop is cultivated on a large scale, especially in the departments of San Miguel and Morazán. The cultivated henequen is used in the larger factories where modern machinery weaves a very good quality of coffee bags, said to be stronger than the imported jute bags used formerly. A modern factory in San Salvador manufactures these bags as well as ropes and cables.

Cotton—This crop has progressed amazingly during the last few years. The greater part is employed for the local weaving industries, which now do not need the imported article. The fight against the bollweevil has had good results. The cotton is hand picked and carefully inspected. Each picker is paid a bonus for each bollweevil he finds. Some of the principal factories are *Mejoramiento Social, La Estrella, San Hilario,* and *Hilandería Salvadoreña.* Besides these well-equipped factories, there are many other looms producing low-priced materials.

Indigo—A quantity of *indigo (añil)* is exported for the Central American textile trade. It was formerly one of the principal export items during the colonial regime, and the Salvadorean *añil* was famous all over the world.

The first treatise on indigo was written by Fray Juan de Dios del Cid about 1741 and entitled *El Puntero Apuntador Con Apuntes Breves.* It was well printed in the hand-set type of that period (see also San Vicente, p. 196).

Domestic trade—First in importance is corn, a food staple for both the high and the low; every section of the country is planted to some corn. It is impossible accurately to figure corn production, because small property holders grow corn for their own use and do not keep statistics.

Beans, especially the so-called black beans *(frijoles),* are a staple grown everywhere in the country. The crop is mostly consumed in the country, with marked preference for the red bean *(frijol colorado).*

Rice and *wheat* are grown to some extent, the latter at the higher altitudes, and both for home consumption only. A greater part of the wheat production is used by the Barcam flour mills, which have modern machinery. *Barcam* is a Pipil word meaning "ground flour."

Tobacco of good quality is raised in small quantities. Nevertheless, most of the tobacco used for manufacturing cigarettes has to be imported.

The *Soya bean (la soja)* is now extensively cultivated for its nutritive value. It is interesting to see how the dry stalks in the cornfields are utilized in August when the corn crop is harvested to serve as supports for the soya plant, which is a vine.

In recent years *el pashte* (Luffa acutangula Curcubitaceas) has been cultivated on a large scale. It is a vine with a large fruit in length fifty or sixty centimeters, cylindrical in form, and when dried of a spongelike quality. It grows on humid land, bearing fruit once a year.

The *cacahuete* or *maní* nut (ground nut) is cultivated on a large scale for the oil of its beans. It bears after four months and as the fruit is underground the land must be dry at the season when the nuts are ripe—in the dry season at the middle of December.

BALSAM

A most famous medicinal product has been erroneously known as Peruvian balsam, when in reality it should be El Salvador balsam. The error originated in Spain over three centuries ago, because the balsam growing in La Costa del Bálsamo in El Salvador was exported from the Pacific coast through Callao, where it joined products from Peru to be reexported to Spain.

The medicinal qualities of balsam were known centuries before the arrival of Columbus. During the early period, the eighth and ninth centuries, the Indians living in the northwestern part of this country, originally from the highlands of Mexico, carried on a brisk trade in balsam, along the coast north to Mexico and down to South America.

The balsam tree (Arbore balsami indici Tolvifera Pereivae Klotszch, Baill, fam. Fabaceae) was first mentioned in history by José de Acosta in 1590, in *Historial Natural y Moral de las Indias*. In 1562 Pope Pius IV and in 1571 Pope Pius V issued briefs authorizing the clergy to use black balsam in the preparation of the chrism.

Two colors are distinguished: the black or very dark brown balsam, and also white balsam having a light, almost transparent yellowish tinge. The white balsam was first prepared by José Eustaquio de León in Guatemala, and used for digestive disorders; it is now known as *Balsamito*. In 1773 the celebrated Sydenham tried this balsam for colics, and used the words "Hunc dolorem afrocisimum sanat balsamum peruvianum frequanter ac in magna deosi exhibitum." When first these products were introduced in Europe, strange properties were attributed to them, and they sold at from $20 to $200 an ounce.

The dry fruit burns easily and has a pleasant odor. The wood is employed along this coast. The trees are ready to be tapped at twenty-five years. In November or December, after the rainy season, the tree is hammered on its four sides with great care, so as to leave the bark intact in four longitudinal places. Then the top layer is removed and the exposed parts are burned with a torch. These are covered with a rough cloth attached to the exposed part through small holes made with a pointed tool. The cloth becomes saturated with the secretion of the tree and when removed and boiled in water the balsam is extracted. After all the balsam has sunk to the bottom of the container, the water is poured out. The balsam obtained by this method is known as *bálsamo de trapo*. Before the cloth is used again, it is wrung out inside a thick net and well twisted.

The balsam known as *bálsamo de cáscara* is obtained by boiling the bark of the tree; commercial balsam is a mixture of the above-mentioned kinds.

Balsam is used for many medicinal purposes: for example, as a digestive stimulant, as a cure for the respiratory ailments and for rheumatism. It is also employed in the manufacture of perfumery. The El Salvador product, which is of the finest quality, must not be confused with other balsams on the market, especially the *Bálsamo de Tolú* of a more tawny color.

During the colonial era the heavy trade in this product brought many galleons to the *Costa del Bálsamo* of Salvador, and there are still traces of that time in the poles with large iron rings to which the galleons were fastened while they were loaded.

The exportation of balsam is considerably reduced at the present time. However, it is used domestically in the manufacture of soap and drugs.

During the colonial period, 1550-1565, diverse Royal

Decrees were issued to help further agriculture in these countries, implements for agriculture were distributed, and special emphasis was placed on the distribution of seeds of all kinds.

INDUSTRIES

Because of its overpopulation El Salvador has had to look for new industries for an outlet for the activities of its people. Therefore, an intense industrialization has developed in all spheres of economic life. Factories large and small have been established or increased in the last decade, so that at the present time Salvadorean manufactured goods compete with and in some cases are better than the imported goods.

Oil—Cottonseed oil is manufactured in a factory known as El Dorado, equipped with the most up-to-date machinery. From the time the cotton is delivered to the last process of clarifying the oil, everything is done with a minimum of effort and a maximum of efficiency. The *Ajonjoli* (sesame seed) and other oil-producing plants are likewise handled here, and experiments are carried on in the adjoining laboratories. The factory has modern sanitation and is surrounded by delightful gardens. A dental clinic adjoins it.

Beer—It is acknowledged that the waters in this country are especially adapted to beer manufacture. The various breweries also provide effervescent waters in different flavors.

Soap—Laundry and toilet soaps made in the country are considered of superior quality. A specialty is the balsam soap, the ingredients for which, and the containers, are essentially the Salvadorean balsam. Also Zapuyul soap made with the zapote fruit is said to be an excellent hair tonic.

Weaving—This industry has progressed amazingly with various types of mechanized looms on which the greater part of the cotton materials used in the country are woven.

Shoes—Salvadoreans are very conscious of their footgear. All classes wear the best shoes they can afford, and few go barefoot. Besides small shoemakers, there are large factories that have a wholesale output of shoes.

Matches—The wood of the country is employed to manufacture matches.

China—A good quality of fancy and ordinary glazed ware for the table and other household uses is also manufactured. Usually the decorations in colors have a very tropical effect.

Glass, Hats, and Candles—These are other flourishing industries, where many workmen are employed and modern machinery has been carefully selected for their manufacture.

Rosarios—A popular small handcraft is the making of the *rosarios* sold at all the big fairs and pilgrimages. Whole families dedicate their days to working on this output; one member spins the threads or fibers, others clean the palm seeds or collect the beads. Another member will string the *rosario,* and finally others will make the attractive silk rosettes that separate the twelve sections. The seed of the Roystonea regia palm is used, washed in hot water before they are colored with the juice of the blackberry. The *rosarios* are blessed by the parish priest before they are put on sale.

Cafe Soluble—In March, 1956, a very modern factory was opened for a new industry, *cafe soluble* or powdered coffee, which already has found a ready market because of its excellent quality.

All small industries exhibit their wares in the warehouses of the *Banco Hipotecario,* where all kinds of handicrafts may be examined and purchased.

The Technological Institute *(Instituto Tecnológico)* investigates the agricultural and industrial life of the country. It is financed in part by the government and in part by private institutions, and is completely autonomous. It contributes data that help in the organization and development of the various agricultural and industrial enterprises in the different regions of the country. The *Instituto de Investigaciones Tropicales* has laboratories that are also a great help to the industries and agriculture.

XVI

FLORA AND FAUNA

MEDICINAL PLANTS

IN A country with such a large percentage of its population living in scattered villages and hamlets without easy access to doctors or hospitals, it is a foregone conclusion that the traditional and inherited knowledge of medicinal plants acquired from their forefathers should be put to use, more than in other less densely populated countries and those with more extensive medical personnel.

Aceituno (Simaruba glauca DC. Simarubaceae). An olive, but not that of Europe and Asia. The bark is used in an infusion for intermittent fevers.

Ala de angel montés (Ruellia geminiflora H.B.K., Acanthaceae). The root is a substitute for ipecacuanha; also a diuretic.

Alhucema or alucena (Hyphis pectinata). The leaves are boiled in water and honey and used to wet a cloth in the shape of a nipple to pacify newborn babies.

Arbol de quina (Coutarea hexandra: Jacq.: Schum, Rubiaceae). Not the well-known Quina or Chinchona. Used when boiled with water for healing wounds.

Artemisa (Ambrosia cumanensis H.B.K. Asteraceae). The boiled flowers are a vermifuge.

Boraja de la tierra (Heliotropium Indicum L., Boraginaceae). The well-mashed leaves dissolve abscesses, boils, and other infections.

Caican (Calea integrifolia C.D. Hemsl. Asteraceae). Used against dandruff.

Capulín Montés (Trema Micrantha L., Blum. Ulmaceae). The bark is used in an infusion against sore throat and mouth sores.

Carey de tortuga (Tortoise shell). Tiny pieces reduced to powder and combined with balsam seeds much used against intestinal pains.

Caulote (Guasuma Ulmifolia Lam., Sterculiaceae). An astringent.

Comemano (Cissus Sicyoides L., Vitaceae). The leaves are used for massaging animals that suffer from rheumatism.

Cuculmeca (Dioscorea Macrostachya Benth, Dioscoreaceae). Stops hemorrhages.

Culantrillo (Adiantum trapeziforme L., Polypodiaceae). A fern used to induce perspiration in fevers, and a good pectoral.

Chipilín (Crotalaria Longirostra Hook & Arn. Fabaceae). The leaves pulverized and mixed with water are a cure for alcoholism. The leaves are likewise used as a condiment for rice and other foods.

Chirca (Thevetia Nerifolia Juss. Apocynaceae). The milky sap from the stalks destroys the roots of decayed teeth.

Euforbio del Monte (Euphorbia Heterophylia L., Euphorbiaceae). For nephritic pains, helping to dislodge calculi. The mashed leaves are used on abscesses and gum boils.

Floripundia (Datura candida Persson Pasq., Solanaceae). Cigarettes made with dried leaves relieve asthma. Flowers placed under the pillow act as a narcotic.

Granadilla Montés (Passiflora platifolia Kilip, Passifloraceae). A diuretic, also used as a refreshing drink, combined with sugar and water.

Guarumo (Cecropia Mexicana Hemsl. Moraceae). From the various species the leaves are ground and boiled with sugar; used for pulmonary troubles. Likewise the toasted leaves reduced to fine powder cure infections.

Hierba hedionda (Cassia Occidentalis L. Caesalinaceae). A tonic, diuretic, vermifuge and used against yellow fever; likewise applied to skin infections and eczema.

Higuerilla, Ricino. (Ricinus Communis L. Euphorbiaceae). The well-known castor oil. Used by the Indians of pre-Columbian days as well as now to soak a piece of cloth at the end of a stick for lighting their huts. Likewise sought as a lubricant and, of course, as a laxative.

Hoja del golpe (Solanum diphyllum L., Solanaceae). The leaves rubbed on bruises lessen pain and prevent inflammation.

Huevo de Tortuga (Physalis pentagona Blake Solanaceae).

Used for dropsy and for leucocythemia following intermittent fevers.

Ishacaca   The Indians use the root of this plant to cure dysentery. It grows abundantly in the vicinity of Chalchuapa.

Malva de las Antillas   (Melochia pyramidata L., Sterculiaceae). The bark and milky substance boiled with sugar and water are used as a vermifuge. The milky substance is used against warts, also prevents traumatic hemorrhages. The leaves when boiled are soothing on sprains.

Manzanita   (Malvaviscus Arboreus Cav. Malvaceae). Soothing for sore throat.

Marañón   (Cashew tree) Anacardium Occidentale L., Anacardiaceae). Toasted nuts are edible. Wine is extracted from the fruit. The shell of the nut is employed to prevent caries of the teeth. Oil Cardol from this tree is a rapid vesicatory. Likewise this oil destroys warts, calluses, and other growths of the skin. The bark is used in baths as an astringent. The concentrated tincture from the bark is efficacious in cases of erysipelas, when affected parts are painted several times a day. The bark also has a tannin content. The almond of the fruit has 40 percent of oil similar to almond oil, used for emulsions. The almond is used for confections, sweets, nougat, syrups, etc. The gum from the bark is used for bookbinding as its bitter taste protects books from the ravages of moths and other insects. Likewise this gum is an excellent varnish for furniture. It is, in fact, a most useful tree whereof every part is available for medicinal or other purposes. There are six known tropical varieties of this tree.

Mata niguas   (Tournefortia volubilis L., Boraginaceae). The mashed leaves applied to infected jigger flea sores kill the insect.

Platanillo   (Canna Indica L., Cannaceae). An infusion of the leaves is a good diuretic.

Pom,   extracted from the copal tree (Protium Copal) used for disinfecting and for incense. Resin used for varnish.

Quiamol   (Entada polystachya L., DC. Momosaceae). The root is used for soap, lotions, and for giving luster to the hair.

Sanguinaria   (Euphorbia Hirta L., Euphorbiaceae). Used internally when the leaves are powdered and boiled in water, and externally the mashed leaves applied to snake bite are supposedly very efficacious.

Tapalayote, or *Friega-Platos* (Solanum Verbasifolium. Solanaceae). The leaves boiled in water are good for kidney and bladder disorders.

The Cocoa-plum of the Americans (Chrysobalanus Icaco L., Amygdalaceae). Used against chronic hemorrhages from the uterus and intestines. The boiled leaves used for baths and local washings and infections.

Verbatan (Gnaphalium attenuatum DC., Asteraceae). Induces perspiration, therefore employed for fevers and coughs. Likewise an emmenagogue and used in a popular antisyphilitic syrup.

Verbena azul (Valerianoides: Stachytarpheta: Mutabile: Jacq.: Kuntze, Verbenaceae). The green leaves boiled in water are an emetic against worms, and the young green leaves are applied to ulcers.

FRUITS

Most tropical fruits are grown in this country and each one of them is delicious, though the stranger must be careful at first not to overeat any of them. The best known are:

Arbol de Pejibaye (Guilielma Utilis Oerst. Phoenicaceae). Delicious fruit, when boiled and used in salads.

Anona Blanca (Annona Diversiflora Salfford. Annonaceae). The well-known custard apple whereof every part of the plant is useful: flowers employed against colds and as an antispasmodic and stomachic. The bark is astringent and used for gastrointestinal infections.

Bananas (Musa sapientium). Many varieties, of which the *plátano* is the best known. Fray Tomás Berlangas, a Dominican, brought the first plant from the Canary Islands to Española in 1516. Later it was brought over to the continental area. It is a question whether the wild banana grew in the forests of South America before the Conquest, as some historians state. Bishop Quiroga, in 1547, was responsible for bringing numerous plants from Sto. Domingo to Mexico, whence they spread south.

Caimito montés (Chrysophyllum Mexicanum Brandley. Sapotaceae). Wild and cultivated *caimitos* are tasty fruits. The bark is medicinal.

Cincuya (Anona Purpurea Moc, & Sessé., Anonaceae). A custard apple whose pulp is a deep orange color; very toothsome.

Coco (Cocos Nucifera L., Phoenicaceae). The coconut is plentiful, and the water of the green fruit much sought for a refreshing drink on the torrid coasts.

Granadilla (Several varieties of this Passifloraceae). The edible fruit is grown on the passion flower vine. Another kind is used for refreshing drinks.

Guayabo (Psidium Guayava L. Myrtaceae). This hardwood tree has the delicious guava fruit.

Guajiniquil—Cujin (Inga Preussi Harms. Mimosaceae). This is a shade tree for coffee plants. The fruit is edible.

Jícama (Pachyrrhizus erosus). The root is a fruit popular in this country. The seed pod, known in the U.S.A. as the yam bean, contains a poison that is used in insecticides.

Jocote Many varieties of this Anacardiaceae fruit. When in season, it is most popular. Looks like a large plum. Medicinally used against chronic dysentery.

Mango (Mangifera indica L., Anacardiaceae). Several varieties on the market during almost the entire year. Originally this tree was brought over in the latter part of the eighteenth century from India.

Oranges and *pineapples* from this country are famous for their sweetness.

Pan de Judea (Artocarpus Communis Moraceae). The well-known breadfruit tree has enormous fruit in this country and is popular sliced and fried, toasted and boiled.

Papaya (Carica Papaya L., Papayaceae. Caricaceae). The paw-paw fruit has pepsin content. Leaves of this tree are used when cooking to soften tough meats.

Paterno (Inga Paterno Harmis. Momosaceae). The fruit contained in the pods is edible.

Pepino (Solanum Muricatum Aiton. Solanaceae). A delicious juicy large plumlike fruit. The name likewise applies to the cucumber.

Pepe-nance (Ximenia Americana L., Olacaceae). A cherrylike fruit. Must be boiled before eating.

Pitaya (Cereus triangularis, fam. Cactáceas). A sweet-tasting and gorgeously colored purple fruit. Indelible stain.

Tamarindo (Tamarindus Indica L., Caesalpinaceae). The fruit pulp is laxative, having citric and tartaric acids. A refreshing drink is made by boiling the fruit; when combined with Cañafístula (Cassia fistula: Caesalpinaceae) is a blood purifier.

Tuna (Opuntia sp. Cactaceae). Also medicinal, for cases of dysentery. Several species.

Zapote (Calopocarpum Mammosum L., Pierre. Sapotaceae). A delicious fruit whose powdered seed and oil are used as a hair tonic.

TREES

Achiote (Bixa Orellana. Bixaceae). The Annatto tree.

Aguacate (Persea gratissima: Lauraceae). A good shade tree. The avocado fruit is of high vitamin value.

Almendro montés (Andiza Jamaicensis Urban, Fabaceae). A splendid hardwood.

Amatle (Ficus sp: Moraceae). Several varieties used as shade trees in village squares.

Bálsamo

Barrillo (Callophyllum Rekoi Standl, Clusiaceae). One of the best woods for buildings.

Ceiba (Ceiba Pentandra L., Rombacaceae). This tall tree is considered sacred by the Indians. A giant of the forest.

Cenizaro (Pithecolobium saman, Benth. Leguminoseae). Wood used for carpentry and cabinetwork, having a fine grain.

Conacaste or *Guanacaste* (Enterolobium cyclocarpum: Mimosaceae). A giant of the forest; its wood used for dugout canoes. The bark is used in an infusion for pulmonary afflictions.

Chapulaltapa (Lonchocarpus Rugosus Benth. Fabaceae). The wood used to make wheels for oxcarts.

Chaperno negro (Lonchocarpus Miniflorus Donn- Smith. Fabaceae). A pretty hardwood tree, whose wood is fine-grained.

Cedro Real (Cedrella Mexicana Roem. C. DC. Maliaceae). The wood has a pleasant odor and is much used for carpentry work.

Copalchi (Croton Reflexifolius. Euphorbiaceae). A much-sought-after wood; the leaves are used to soothe headaches.

Castaño (Sterculia Apetala Jacq. Karst. Staphylaceae). Not to be taken as the European hazel tree. The white wood is used for making boxes for soap and candles. The seeds are used as a purgative.

Cicahuite (Lysiloma Acapulcense Kuntz. Benth, Momosaceae). A hardwood tree with very fine grain.

Flor de la Cruz (Plumeria Alba Fam. Apocinaceaes). Not a large tree, having spectacular red and white flowers, used to decorate altars during the feast of La Cruz on May 2 and 3. The sap from the tender branches has an excellent 4 percent rubber content.

Guachipilín (Diphysa Robinoides Benth. Fabaceae). A hardwood used for buildings and railroad ties.

Huilihuiste (Karwinskia Calderoni Standl. Rhamnaceae). A good construction wood.

Mangle (Rhizophora Mangle L., Rhizophoraceae). Mangrove tree, the light wood of which turns a deep red when exposed to the air. Hardwood used for dugouts and small boats. The bark is used for tanning leather.

Madre Cacao (Gliricidia sepim: Fabaceae). "Mother Cacao," a tree used to shade the coffee tree. Its poisonous roots drive away insect pests. Spectacular during its flowering season.

Matilisqua (Tabebuia pentaphylla: Bignomiaceae). Light yellow wood popular for cabinetwork. Spectacular flowering season when it sheds its leaves.

Palo Mora (Chlorophora Tinctoria L., Guad. Moraceae). Furniture wood having an artistic orange tinge, which, when exposed to the air, turns pale yellow. This is prevented by a good varnish. Also used for oxcart wheels. Supplies an excellent dye.

Morro (Crescentia alata and Crescentia Cujete: Bignoniaceae). Its fruit is used to make gourds.

Quina or *Cinchona* (Cinchona officinalis: Rubiaceae). The well-known quinine tree from which this medicine is extracted.

Tecomasuche (Cochlospermum vitifalium: Cochlospermaceae). A spectacular tree when in flower, having large yellow blossoms and small gourd-like fruit used for medicinal purposes.

Tempisque (Sideroxylon Tempisque, Pittier. Sapotaceae). The wood is white and looks well when varnished.

Shila (Bombax aequaticum). The Aztecs called it Xiloxochitl or Toloxcoc, meaning "flower like the corn cob." Five leaves grow on a stemlike hand, and appear after the flowers drop in May. The flowers look toward heaven and only when faded do they look toward earth and drop at 10 o'clock at night, covering the ground with a bloodlike rain. Children and grownups gather the flowers to decorate their hair, and attribute mystic qualities to them. In this country the Indians call it Xila. The wood is used for wooden wash-trays (baleas); the bark is used medicinally for diabetes.

Uvilla This small tree is unique inasmuch as it is covered continually with a dark grapelike fruit that the inhabitants of this region, San José del Chagüite, department of La Unión, use combined with honey to make a very palatable wine.

Izote (Yucca elephantipes). When the tree is pruned to a twelve-ft. height, the roots develop and prevent soil erosion in hilly terrain. The flowers cooked in egg batter are a popular food.

BIRDS

El Salvador has only a limited range of birds that might be classified as neotropical, as it is crowded between the Pacific Ocean and the range of mountains bordering thereon.

Most of the bird species are migratory, wintering in the south; they arrive in September or October, and go north again in March or April. About fifteen species of Spelerpes have been classified from Central America.

Birds—Among the owls are the white owl, the great horned owl or Bubo, and the tiny owls distinguished by their eartufts. Scops owls are confined to the region of the San Miguel volcano. In the region of La Libertad the spectacle owls are plentiful. Occasionally in remote regions the bare-toed owls may be found.

The osprey is found in the lagoons and along the coast.

The black buzzard (*zopilote* or black vulture of Mexico) is abundant all over the country. At sea level and sometimes at higher elevations, the red-headed turkey vulture appears.

In fresh-water lagoons and forest swamps there is a bird resembling the fish-hawk. Near La Libertad are several kinds of hawks, particularly the rain crow, so called because of its peculiar cry, which has earned for it also the name of "laughing hawk." The duck-hawk breeds in the cliffs on the coast of Acajutla, but belongs to the migratory birds. The *quiebrahueso, caracara,* or bone-breaker hawk is plentiful in this same region.

Pelicans breed on the islands of the Bay of Fonseca; they are winter visitors together with the herons, night-heron storks, spoonbills, and ibis in this region. Every so often an *alcatraz* (albatross) may be seen on the coast flying south, but it rarely rests in these latitudes. Flamingoes, white and pink, camp on the banks of rivers and swamps; they cannot be compared to the well-known flamingoes of other parts of the world.

Many kinds of swans, ducks, and geese, particularly the muscovy duck, are found. The black-bellied tree-ducks haunt the cornfields during the night. Their peculiar whistle has given them the name "whistling duck." The teal-duck or blue-winged teal is a winter visitor, and comes early to the region of the Bay of Fonseca.

Several different species of pigeons are found, the red-billed pigeon in the region of San Miguel volcano, the band-tailed pigeon and the Inca dove around La Libertad; the small ground-dove lives along the Pacific Coast, and larger ones near La Libertad.

This country has many good game birds; partridge, snipe, quail, and pheasant make for good hunting.

Another winter migrant is the coot, a rail-like aquatic bird. The whimbrels are found in the Bay of Fonseca. The spotted sandpiper winters near La Libertad. The jacanas, tropical wading birds, plovers, sand-pipers, the turnstone— a plover-like bird, so called because it turns over the stones to look for its food—and the kildeer plover, known by this name because of its peculiar cry—all these birds are found on the islands of the Bay of Fonseca.

The tern, a bird resembling a quail, especially the American black tern, and the small tern are found along the coast. Another winter migrant is the catbird, or cat thrush, so called because of its catlike cry. The flycatcher, the rock-wren, and wrenlike birds are found near La Unión and the Conchagua Volcano, at an altitude of four thousand feet. The summer warbler of the U.S.A. and the Blackburnian warbler spend the winter near La Libertad, as does also a small bird much like a flycatcher. The indigo bird of North America is found at La Unión.

Swallows are found at La Unión and on the islands of the Bay of Fonseca, orioles along the coast, and the barn swallow around stables. Jays are numerous, likewise various kinds of hummingbirds, blackbirds, and a small thrushlike diving bird, the dipper; also bluebirds and tits.

Ant-thrushes, as well as the cuckoo, sometimes called *pájaro ardilla* or squirrel bird, and the ground-cockoos, sometimes called pijijes, haunt streams and swamps. There seem to be innumerable species of cuckoos.

Central America is endowed with thirty-four species belonging to ten genera of parrots; the red- and blue-headed macaws are found near La Libertad; and there are parakeets of many kinds, as well as the short-tailed parrots, a variety of tiny green parrots, and the parrot with a yellow nape, supposedly a good talker.

MAMMALS

The most striking mammals are the monkeys: the spider monkey, the marmosets, the white-throated Capuchín, and several common species in the thickly wooded sections of the country. There are bats, especially the brown bat, as well as an occasional vampire bat and the Macrotus bat, a large bat having a harsh screech, which is well recognized. The wrinkled-faced bat is the most hideous of all. Shrews are also found, though they are not numerous. The jaguar, erroneously called *tigre,* lives in El Salvador. The *manigordo,* ocelot, is the most beautiful of the cat tribe. Occasionally a puma, erroneously called *león,* is found. The coyote too is found, mistaken for the wolf, though scientists explain its presence with coincident importation of European cattle. and therefore is not indigenous. Several kinds of common raccoons are found in some sections, as well as the white-nosed coati (*pizote*), the *micoleón,* the kinkajou, in addition to the weasel, skunk, badger, though the latter are rare.

Tapirs—*danta*—live near the Gulf of Fonseca, and the pec-

cary (*coche de monte*). Many deer are in the forests, and
very small deer along the Pacific Coast.

There are many squirrels of all kinds; porcupines are
rare; the agouti is found and *tepeizcuinte,* a fine-flavored
game animal, hares, sloths, armadillos and anteaters of various kinds; opossum, and water-opossum (*el tacuazin de agua*
or *zorro de agua*).

LEPIDOPTERA

Moths and butterflies are both known in the Spanish
language as *Mariposas.* There is no available study about
Salvadorean Lepidoptera; some information is contained in
the English translation of the *Macro-Lepidoptera of the
World* by the scientist Zeits. An unbelievably unexplored
field for the student and collector is found in every section
of the country, but especially at low altitudes.

Of the moths, the Arsenura (arcaef-Pachygonia ribbei) is
perhaps the best known; it is considered a harbinger of bad
luck, or as one person stated, "it contained the spirit of a dear
departed and therefore must not be killed."

Three well-known species of the brownish black moth of
the Psychidea family inhabit the lowlands in every section
of the country. Innumerable species of the Morpho butter-
fly, considered the most beautiful in the world, may be
found at all altitudes and add their spectacular colors to the
tropical landscape, together with literally thousands of other
varieties which await a scientist's proper classification and
extensive study.

AQUATIC AND OTHER LIFE

Fishes may be divided into two classes: those belonging to
the fresh-water rivers, inland lakes, lagoons, and pools, and
those tropical shore fishes that enter rivers.

Good fishing of all kinds is afforded in the Gulf of Fonseca. Among the fresh-water fishes is the delicate *robalito*
(small Robalo of the family Centropomidae). Sea fish found
are pipe fish, the perchlike fishes, blackfish, sea bass, flying

fish, swordfish, the mullet, the lampreys, mackerel of the tropical seas and fresh-water localities. One species, Poecilia salvatoris, a fish fifty-five millimeters in length, is peculiar to these waters. Fresh-water eels travel to the sea for mating. Catfish, carp, and the ever-present sharks of tropical waters are found, and the *boca colorada* (red-mouth fish), which is an excellent food fish.

Turtles, crocodiles, and *alligators* abound. Large lizards, especially iguanas, are in most of the rivers and inlets. Lizards measuring three inches without the tail are found in the region of La Unión, and a tiny variety of lizard in other parts. Near Cuzcatlán there is a horned lizard. The chameleons and salamanders are more plentiful in the eastern regions, where they destroy vermin in houses.

Frogs of all kinds are plentiful. There is an interesting variety of tree frog, whose female has no dorsal pouch. There is also a tiny turtle not more than three and a half inches long and seldom more than two inches.

Snakes—Both poisonous and non-venomous snakes are numerous, of many varieties, and found in all parts of the country. Sea snakes are seldom found. The *masacuata,* though not poisonous, is interesting because of its large size and the spots that make it appear like a deer, hence the name: deer snake, *masat-coatl.*

Centipedes and roaches are household pests in the more congested regions.

The Central American mamalian fauna seems to be a mixture of the North and South American. Frederick Ducane Godman in *Biologia Centrali-Americana* states that "the intermingling and cross migrations seem to have started the Miocene age."

The above is a too-brief survey of only a few of the hundreds of interesting birds, mammals, fishes, and reptiles of El Salvador.

XVII

THE LANDSCAPE OF EL SALVADOR

BAYS

THE picturesque *Bay of Fonseca* was known to the Indians as Chorotega. Parts of it belong to the republics of Nicaragua and Honduras; that belonging to El Salvador, called Bahía de La Unión, has two ports: Cutuco and La Unión. It is divided into two bays, with one deep and one narrow channel; the first is called Bocana de Chiquirín. The entrance to the bay is thirty-five kilometers at its narrowest point, and on the Salvadorean side has a lighthouse on Point Chiquirín (Chiquirín is a small shrimplike animal, so called by the Nicaraguans). This bay was named for the Spanish prelate, Juan Rodríguez de Fonseca, Bishop of Burgos (1451-1524), whose machinations caused turmoil in the conquest schemes of America.

At all times this bay has been coveted as an entrance to a many times projected transcontinental canal connecting the Atlantic and the Pacific oceans. Great Britain saw in such a canal a splendid opportunity for aggrandizement, and maneuvered to accomplish it. Her schemes were almost successful, when a detachment of the British Pacific squadron with Her Majesty's Consul General in Guatemala appeared in this bay and took possession of the five principal islands in the name of the British Crown. President Taylor of the U.S.A. appointed as Minister to Central America E. G. Squier, who countered this maneuver by arranging with the Government of Honduras the cession of the largest island to the U.S.A. This stopped the British scheme, and the Clayton-Bulwer Treaty including recognition of the position of the United States, was signed between the two great powers on April 19, 1850.

This bay has been from time immemorial a strategic place of refuge for pirates and marauders who were carrying on their depredations in the neighboring countries.

The principal islands belonging to El Salvador are Meanguera, Conchaguita, Martín Pérez, and Punta Zacate, whereon good drinking water may be found. Smaller islands are Chuchito, Meanguerita, Irca, Perico, Conejo, and Camarín. This bay is a fisherman's paradise with quantities of different varieties of fish.

The *Bay of Jiquilisco*, situated between the mouths of the Lempa and Río Grande de San Miguel rivers, is a scenic spot with a small port called Guachaguantique, where fishermen have huts. The port of *El Triunfo* or *Espíritu Santo* on this bay was in use from 1829 on, but was abandoned recently. This bay has several islands: Espíritu Santo, Corral de Mulas, and San Sebastián. In the bay at El Triunfo the depth never is less than twelve feet at low tide and twenty-two at high tide.

The *Estero de Jaltepeque*, in the department of La Paz, is sixty-one kilometers from San Salvador on a paved highway; it has a port, La Concordia, but a dangerous bar prevents its use. This estuary is picturesque and measures over ninety kilometers from the mouth of Río Guajoyo to La Barra de Escalante on the west.

The *Bay of Mizata* was utilized as the entrance to the port of the same name during colonial days, and still offers possibilities of transformation into a good port for large-sized vessels.

RIVERS

About three hundred sixty large rivers and three hundred fifty smaller ones cross the territory of this country:

	Kilometers	
Lempa, also known as Atlempa	300	
Río Grande de San Miguel	72	Navigable by small craft
Jiboa	70	
Río de Paz	56	

The river *Lempa* rises near the village of Esquipulas in Guatemala; as it gathers waters, it forms a formidable stream before it enters the Pacific Ocean. It has a river port, La Barca. During the week before Holy Week, fishermen with their respective families camp on the banks, fish during the day, and at night dry the fish over large campfires.

At the place where the *Río Grande de San Miguel* enters the Pacific Ocean it forms La Isla del Arco, a popular sea-bathing resort. It springs from the southwest slopes of the Cacahuatique Hills.

The clear waters of the *Rio de Paz* are not good for drinking, because of the saline elements which seep from the thermal springs of the nearby Sierra de Apaneca. It is part of the boundary line between Guatemala and this country, and enters the Pacific Ocean.

The *Jiboa* originates at the back of the hill Las Delicias near San Rafael Los Cedros, and its waters are augmented by the outlet of Lake Ilopango.

The *Goascorán* is the boundary between the Republic of Honduras and El Salvador, and is crossed by the Pan American Highway.

Among the smaller rivers of interest is *El Carrizal*, near Dulce Nombre de María village, in the department of Chalatenango, where there is a natural tunnel in the rock, forty meters long by eight meters wide.

The river *Huisquilapa* in the department of La Paz has on its bank the geyser El Castaño, which popular legend claims has very hot water in the morning and very cold water in the afternoon. The *Anguiatu* is a river as well as the name of an outlying village on the railroad line between Guatemala and El Salvador. The word means "Bedbug of the reed mat." Owing to the broken ground of the country, most of the rivers form scenic waterfalls and pools which are used for swimming.

LAKES

Numerous lakes dot the country and during the rainy season their number is augmented by the rain pools, often large and deep. The most important larger lakes are:

Lake Güija, thirty kilometers long by ten kilometers wide and fifty meters deep. It is situated partly in Guatemala and partly in the department of Santa Ana. It is an interesting sheet of water, having vestiges of a pre-Columbian civilization, which can be seen at the bottom on a clear day. The fishermen use typical dugouts *(balsas)* with a boxlike superstructure. The principal island is the volcanic cone, La Isla. The Indian name Cuixin-Atl or Güija means "water hawk." The Indians in the vicinity of this lake have a curious custom: in the week before Holy Week they catch alligators, which abound in the lake, and take them to a nearby hamlet, where the only building that is not a thatched hut is the Alcaldía, combined with the school and prison. The latter boasts a room with a barred door. The leader of the fishermen convinces the *Alcalde* that he and his followers must be locked in the prison room. The big village drum is beaten and as by magic hordes of Indians emerge and congregate in the square. They gather around the prison door, hand in a few cents through the bars, and receive in exchange luscious titbits of alligator meat, which they then and there devour raw.

Lake Ilopango, thirteen by nine kilometers, lies at an altitude of 442 meters; it is sixteen kilometers east of the capital city and twelve hundred feet lower than the city. The lake is of a volcanic nature. In 1880, a seismic disturbance caused a small volcano to form almost in the center of the lake, killing the fish. Now this volcano has risen to one hundred seventy feet and adds to the scenic beauty of the lake. The waters periodically rise and recede. The lake is a favorite for boating, swimming, and all kinds of water sports. Asino, a port situated on this lake, is located north of Santiago Texacuangos. Apulo on Lake Ilopango is a modern resort with good fishing, and is very popular on Sundays.

Lake Coatepeque, department of Santa Ana, has a surface of forty square kilometers and is four hundred feet deep. It is a beautiful sheet of water encircled by high hills. The shores have many attractive cottages, and all kinds of water sports are enjoyed on the lake. Two peninsulas point into the lake, El Pedregal and Apela, twin hills of pumice stone, black obsidian with feldspar out of which a constant vapor cloud issues. From here the hot water springs flow. The islands of El Cabro or Cedro Grande (two hundred fifty feet above the lake), and San Pedro add to the picturesque aspect of the spot. Good roads communicate with the most important centers in the country. The nearby village of El Congo provides supplies and is a railroad station.

Lake Olomega, department of San Miguel, is of volcanic origin, with a surface of approximately sixty-five square kilometers. It is very rich in many species of fish and alligators, and its banks are the home of water fowl: wild ducks, egrets, flamingoes, and other tropical birds. A railroad station in the nearby village of Olomega provides a small hotel.

Atecozol, meaning pleasant water, is the name of a lovely bathing spot near Izalco in the department of Sonsonate. It has a gorgeous setting amid tropical surroundings, with views of the country and the nearby Izalco volcano.

Lake Apastepeque, department of San Vicente, is near the modern Pan American Highway. It also has beautiful views, good fishing and boating.

Among the smaller lakes the best known are *Chanmico,* in the department of La Libertad, with good fishing and very deep waters, and *Chalchuapa,* also with many varieties of tropical fish and water fowl. It is located four kilometers east of San Esteban Catarina, department of San Vicente.

POPULAR RESORTS AND THERMAL SPRINGS

The beaches of *Los Blancos y Los Negros* are popular summer bathing places on the Estero de Jaltepeque.

El Pimental, department of La Paz, is a popular bathing beach on the Pacific Coast near a small village.

La Toma, one mile distant from Quezaltepeque, has large mineral springs with two well-constructed swimming tanks. The springs pour from a rocky lava formation, and the place is famous as the Vichy of El Salvador, because of the medicinal properties of its waters for diabetes and arthritis, rheumatism, and related ailments. Analysis of the water is as follows:

	Grams per Liter		*Grams per Liter*
Sulphuric acid	0.035	Carbonic acid	0.947
Silica	0.104	Hydrochloric acid	0.009
Lime	0.057	Dry extracts	9.473
Magnesia	0.030	Organic matter	trace
Soda	0.005		

Lake Coatepeque, mentioned above, has waters with qualities considered effective for digestive troubles. The bottled water is sold everywhere in the country:

	Grams per Liter
Bicarbonate of calcium	0.046
Sulphate of calcium	0.089
Sulphate of magnesia	0.076
Sulphate of potassium	0.087
Sulphate of sodium	0.085
Chloride of sodium	0.502

The Ausoles near Ahuachapán have thermal springs with waters splendid for rheumatism and arthritis. The waters are sulphurous with a temperature of 100° C. Other thermal springs with the same name are by the River Tilapa (San Pedro Masahuat).

At *Los Chorros,* formed by the River El Guarumal, are good bathing facilities. Also known as *Agua Caliente,* these baths are near Santa Tecla and the waters have medicinal qualities.

Chiquirín, also known as *La Playa del Encanto,* is a good bathing beach near La Unión.

El Agua Caliente, hot springs five kilometers north of Quezaltepeque.

El Coro, thermal springs southeast of San Salvador.

El Infiernillo del Jute and *El Infiernillo del Obrajuelo* are thermal springs eight kilometers from Agua Caliente, department of Chalatenango.

La Laguna or *Lagunea,* hot springs with excellent public baths, near Tenancingo, and *El Cacao,* with good bathing facilities and very hot water are in the department of Cuzcatlán.

El Mango is a sea-bathing beach near Jucuarán, department of Usulután.

La Mina, radioactive springs, are one kilometer from Sensuntepeque.

Los Baños, medicinal springs with bathing tanks are in San Rafael, department of Chalatenango.

Los Borbollones, hot springs much frequented after the Feria de Ceniza (Ash Fair) are in San Ramón, department of Cuzcatlán.

Shuteca, thermal medicinal waters near the river of this name are east of Nahuilingo, department of Sonsonate.

MOUNTAINS AND VOLCANOES

Mountains and volcanoes are not important because of their height but spectacular because of the number of volcanoes within this small territory, which have caused constant upheavals:

Peak	Department	Height, meters	
Cojutepeque	Cuzcatlán	1,021	
Cerro Verde	Usulután	1,555	
Conchagua	La Unión	1,250	At entrance of La Unión Bay.
Cuyutepeque	Ahuachapán	1,600	

Peak	Department	Height, meters	
Chinameca	San Miguel	1,402	Crater 2 kilometers wide, erroneously called Laguna del Pacayal, as it is fertile land, not a lake.
Chichicastepeque or Apaneca	Ahuachapán	1,454	
El Limbo	San Miguel	1,400	Ancient crater on summit
Guazapa	San Salvador	1,411	
Izalco	Sonsonate	1,885	
Jucuapa	Usulután	1,658	Six peaks and thermal springs.
Santa Ana or Ilamatepec	Santa Ana	2,385	
San Jacinto	San Salvador	1,171	
San Miguel or Chaparrastique	San Miguel	2,132	Worst eruption in 1787, with lava flow now known as *La Malpaicera*
San Salvador	San Salvador	1,950	
San Vicente or Chichontepec	San Vicente	2,173	
Usulután	Usulután	1,453	Two craters. No historical record of eruptions.

A spectacular range in the western zone of the Republic is known as the Izalco group, having Cerro Grande de Apaneca as its highest summit, a basaltic rock of volcanic nature without a crater. Near the town of Apaneca is Cerrito de Apaneca with a very shallow crater on the northeast side and a deeper one on the south side. The Lagunita volcano has a lake at the bottom of the crater, which supplies the village of Apaneca with water. The lake is at an altitude of 6,574 feet. Next to it is the Laguna Verde volcano, with Green

Lake in the crater bottom. Farther toward the northeast are the peaks of the Cuyanansul or San Juan Heights, with geysers and fumaroles. Toward the east of this peak are four practically unexplored peaks: Las Aguilas, Tamagastepec, La Laguna de la Rana with a lake in the center, and Mala Cara. Toward the south is the Volcán Naranjo.

The Izalco volcano, known as *El Faro Centro Americano,* the Central American Lighthouse, is the most interesting of this group. The inhabitants in the vicinity heard noises like thunder proceeding from a rock on the south slope of the Santa Ana volcano. Thunderlike rumblings continued, the earth shook continually until a tremendous upheaval opened up the earth, and a small hill or volcano was formed; this continued to grow until the imposing volcano of the present time was formed. Since February 23, 1770, it has been most active, and more than once has threatened the villagers beneath its shadow. The last eruption in 1926 caused a wide current of lava to descend toward the Izalco village. It is an imposing sight to watch the constant eruption at regular five-minute intervals, as stones, smoke, and fire are thrown into the air to great heights. This has given it the name of Central American Lighthouse because navigators on the Pacific shores watch for the illumination as they cruise north and south.

The *Santa Ana* is the largest of this group. Vestiges of an ancient crater to the east of the present one and a circular crater with a creek separating it from a smaller oval crater are interesting. A small river descends into Agua Shuca Lake, so named because of its greenish waters. This volcano seemingly was most active during the years of the Conquest. Oidor Palacios mentions violent eruptions in 1576. The eruptions of 1847 and 1880 were disastrous, that of 1880 covering the nearby lands with four feet of ashes, ruining crops, and killing cattle. Again in 1904 and 1937 there were signs of activity, but fortunately the eruption was mild, with smoking fumaroles and geysers issuing nearby. The slopes are intensively cultivated in coffee plantations. A secondary peak on the eastern slope known as La Loma Redonda is not active.

The *San Salvador* volcano, on whose lap the capital city is located, has a cone on the northern border of the crater, and at the bottom of the crater there used to be a picturesque lake. In 1917 it was drained by a strong seismic disturbance. On the southwest slope the cone El Jabalí caused a violent eruption in June, 1917.

The volcanic range of San Vicente has as its highest point the *San Vicente* volcano, and has in the same group *Usulután* volcano. The Volcán Tecapa in the Algería Hills has geysers and hot springs. Also of this group is El Taburete, which has the shape of a stool, hence its name.

In the middle of the country there is another volcanic group having the volcanic peaks Chingo, Guazapa, Cacaguatique, and Sociedad.

The *San Miguel* volcano has from time immemorial had awe-inspiring eruptions. The worst recorded were in 1787 and 1844. This region boasts many miles of lava fields, some more ancient than others; the older ones have some vegetative cover of the grim black mass.

In this region the Chinameca has an enormous crater two kilometers wide, which for no apparent reason is called "Laguna del Pacayal"; instead of a lagoon, it is very fertile agricultural land. It is also known as "El Boquerón." The Volcán Siguatepeque or Ciguatepec on the right bank of the River Lempa has no historical record of eruptions, but during the heavy seismic disturbances all over this country in 1936, rumblings were heard and quakes were felt.

El Playón is a volcanic hill, and south of this is a good-sized plain covered with pumice stone. In 1659, in September, a lava flow descended on the northeast side, destroying plantations and ruining the town of Nejapa. The population barely escaped by a narrow trail before the lava closed in on all sides.

XVIII

ARCHAEOLOGICAL SITES, MINES, AND CAVES

ARCHAEOLOGICAL SITES

WHEREVER the soil is disturbed in El Salvador, archaeological remains are found. Even in the center of the capital city numerous ceramics have been dug up, particularly on the Zapote Hill. A couple of years ago the Carnegie Institution of Washington started studies in this country, which are being continued in the region of the department of Ahuchapán, the ruins of Tazumal. Under the direction of the Tulane University Museum of New Orleans, excavations are also being carried on in San Andrés, department of La Libertad. At *Jujutla*, department of Ahuachapán, on the island of El Cajete in the River Paz, are found prehistoric stoneworks, a temple of stone resembling Toltec or perhaps Aztec pre-Columbian ruins.

At *Zincantlán*, department of La Libertad, at Las Flores are pre-Columbian ruins.

At *Xalpa*, on the Costa del Bálsamo, there is a unique monolith with undeciphered inscriptions. The inhabitants call it La Piedra del Sol.

At *Tehuacán*, department of San Vicente, and *Atehuan*, department of La Libertad are pre-Columbian sites yielding human remains, mounds, and ceramics. The word *Atehuan* is significant, meaning "strangers," and perhaps refers to pre-Columbian migrants who settled on this spot.

Isla de Igualtepeque, in Lake Güija, department of Santa Ana, has most interesting ruins, stelae, and pyramids. This region must have been the scene of tremendous seismic

147

cataclysms submerging the islands in this lake with their buildings. The smaller island of Teotipa also shows a pre-Columbian occupancy.

At *Quelepa,* department of San Miguel, three different civilizations seem to have occupied the vast plain in the vicinity of the San Miguel River. The ceramics are unique, different from those found in other parts of the country.

At *Cihuatán,* department of San Salvador, the ruins are located on top of a hill, with traces of a place of sacrifice, a pyramid with steps on its four sides, a plaza with innumerable mounds; many hills with ruins are scattered over this region. The principal pyramid is supposedly from 2,000 to 2,500 years old. The ceramics are worth studying as they bear a resemblance to those of Aztec civilizations.

At *Jacaltepeque,* department of San Vicente, the ruins are situated on the slopes of the Jacaltepeque hill. History says that the Indian confederation under the chief of Tehuacán scattered, and part of them established themselves on the slopes near the estuary of Jacaltepeque or Jaltepeque, where the islands have remains of ancient civilizations.

Four kilometers to the northeast of *Juayua,* department of Sonsonate, on the estate of San Luis, there are quantities of mounds.

At *Acajutla,* department of Sonsonate, two interesting figurines (now at the Museum in the Archbishop's palace in the capital) were found on the eastern hill at a depth of three meters. These figures are different from any pre-Columbian art found up to now in Central America. Who brought them to this site or what civilization made them is a puzzle.

Pictographs denote an ancient civilization, as already mentioned. Perhaps the best known is *La Piedra Pintada,* in the department of La Libertad. Here there is a huge monolithic stone five meters high with another stone forming a rooflike structure overhanging and protecting the hieroglyphs incised and painted in red. This stone stands at the end of a deep ravine about ten miles from the coast, and was probably a shelter for marauders who left these glyphs to tell their followers the story of their adventures.

San Andrés. These ruins are in a plantation on the Pan Américan Highway. Pyramids indicate that this place was a very important center—two of the pyramids have been restored.

The ruins of *Tazumal* are spectacular. The large pyramids have steps leading up to the top. Buildings still to be seen have various inscriptions and carvings denoting a very ancient civilization. The famous *Virgen de Tazumal* often mentioned in Salvadorean literature has lately been studied and declared to not be the figure of a female, but the stone figure of a male. These ruins are situated to the southeast of the central plaza of the town of Chalchuapa and are imposing and extensive. The place has been well reconstructed, with a small museum at one side. It is accessible from Chalchuapa and not far from Santa Ana.

MINES

This country is exceptionally rich in minerals. Some have been mined, and others offer possibilities to the enterprising prospectors.

I mention a few of the principal mines, such as:

Caparrosa, on the banks of the Agua Fría River, department of Chalatenango.

El Aguacate, department of Cabañas.

El Divisadero, department of Morazán.

El Gigante, department of Morazán.

El Hormiguero, department of San Miguel.

La Mina, department of Chalatenango, located on a high hill.

La Montañita, department of Chalatenango, a silver mine.

Las Charcas, department of La Unión.

Tinta Amarilla and *Las Piñas,* department of La Unión.

Cerro de la Mina (hill of the mines), department of Chalatenango, a gold mine.

Chacalpita, department of San Salvador, supplies white gypsum, and *El Jiote,* department of San Miguel, produces gypsum of many colors.

Los Axumes, department of Santa Ana, is a gold mine and has mercury veins as well.

El Cerro Pacho, department of Cabañas, has copper deposits.

INTERESTING CAVES

Natural phenomena occur in various parts of the country and are well worth the visitor's interest:

The cave of *Chinchinaga,* department of La Paz, is famous because of the belief that it was the site where Nahuatl Indian witch doctors practiced their crafts. The name means "Cave of Torments."

Laguna Escondida cave, department of La Libertad, has pictographs on its rock walls.

La Batueca, a curious ravine in the department of San Vicente, shows recent geological changes. During 1936 it opened a crevice wherefrom a spring and large waterfall issued. This place has sulphur and gypsum mines.

La Campana (the bell), department of Cuzcatlán, is so called because when knocked the rock walls give forth a clear bell-like sound.

La Leona, department of Cabañas, is a cave having a deep and stony entrance. Legend attributes to this site a great hidden treasure left by the bandit El Partideño.

La Periquera, department of La Libertad, is eight kilometers distant from Santa Tecla. A river and scenic waterfall spring from it.

Las Cárceles, department of Santa Ana, is a succession of caves having bars like a prison. It is formed by a brook of the same name.

El Hermitaño, department of Chalatenango, has indecipherable red figures on its walls.

Gruta de Corinto, department of Morazán, has numerous queer human figures in red, blue, and yellow painted on its rock walls.

Las Torrecillas, department of La Unión, are rocklike towers. At their feet is a large cave, which looks like a door.

The bathing resort at Atecozol, at the foot of Izalco Volcano.

*The countryside. Above is a view of the mountains from Ichanmichen Na-
tional Park; below is the churchyard in Panchimalco.*

The city. The upper view shows the National Palace in San Salvador; the
lower shows some modern buildings in the commercial part of San Salvador.

The country. A general view of the landscape.

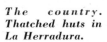

The country. Thatched huts in La Herradura.

The people. Three women of Nahuizalco.

Above is El Pilar Church in San Vicente, designed and begun in 1762. Right is a Holy Week celebration in Sonsonate. The "carpets" are made of sawdust.

Above, the old colonial church at Panchimalco. Below, a Salvadorean woman selling hats in the market.

A coffee bloom.

The monument to the fathers of Salvadorean independence.

Legends are woven around this place, and the people do not like to go near it.

Los Magüeyes, department of San Vicente. This is a large cave located on the borders of the Juñapa River; twenty-five persons can easily be accommodated therein. During the rainy season fishermen and hunters take refuge in this cave.

Letrero del Diablo (The Writing of the Devil), department of La Libertad; *Las Tres Piedras,* department of La Unión; and *La Peña del Diablo,* department of La Unión, are caves with pre-Columbian pictographs and figures painted in red.

Puertas de Obomba, department of Morazán, are intriguing caves worth visiting.

San Juan Talpa, department of La Paz, also known as *Apancinte,* is associated by popular legend with magic manifestations and is therefore feared.

El Ujushtal, Los Tamales, and *El Zapotal* are three large caves in a queerly shaped hill in the department of Sonsonate. The last named has a deep lagoon.

Cueva de la Vieja is formed by rock and lava formations; the superstitious believe that in this cave lives a sinister spirit, guarded by hordes of mosquitoes who prevent the entrance of strangers.

XIX

THE CAPITAL, SAN SALVADOR

THE modern capital of the Republic is something unique among Central American capitals. It has passed through so many catastrophes of nature and mankind that it is surprising to the visitor to see the present up-to-date and busy city. Literally, one might say that it is not only a phœnix, but a nestful of them that have risen from the many times ruined and despoiled city to achieve its present status. Situated in the department of San Salvador, it lies at an elevation of 682 meters on the slopes of the San Salvador volcano and the western slope of San Jacinto Hill. The population is 164,566.

The frequent destructions and reconstructions account for the lack of colonial-style buildings as well as the many gaps in buildings that as yet have not been reconstructed since the last catastrophe. Nevertheless, the last decade has seen enormous changes. The modern city has become the center of all activities in the Republic. It has well-paved streets, the concrete and steel of modern architecture have been combined to build houses to resist earthquakes, and its beautiful gardens are the pride of their owners. Some of the best club buildings in the Isthmus are the gathering places for society. Sport clubs, parks, and government buildings add their attractions to a very modern and transformed city.

The former colonial houses with their large patio style of architecture are rapidly being replaced by the modern chalet or by villas built on the surrounding hills. These *colonias* are picturesque, and it is in the *colonias* that modern San Salvador is at its cool best. The principal ones are Mejicanos,

Parque Modelo, Planes de Renderos, La Doble Vía, Colonia Dueñas, Lomas de Candelaria, Colonia San Benito, Colonia América, Colonia Flor Blanca, Colonia El Zapote, the last on the San Jacinto Hill. One with an Indian name, Amatepeque, meaning "mountain of the amate trees," is located on the southeast of the city, where a fort, the presidential residence and a museum are situated.

The colonial period added churches of the various orders and convents, of which scant vestiges remain at present.

The city, always a gay place, has become renowned for its hospitality and its readiness to share its many gaieties with the stranger within its gates. Money and good spirits are never lacking to welcome the stranger, and it is perhaps the only capital in Central America where foreigners are admitted to the inner social circles without restraint.

The city is divided by the River Acelhuate; the name means *Agua de la hierba tierna* (water of the young weed).

PARKS

Parks and small gardens dot the city as becomes a tropical climate, where the torrid hours of midday drive everyone to seek cool shade. Life stirs in the wee hours of morning; everyone takes a siesta or rest during the warmest part of the day. The nights are cool throughout the year, and the months of December and January are cool and agreeable.

El Campo de Marte is a delightful park on the western side of the city. Here there are beautiful lawns, large shade trees that bloom satisfyingly during the months of March and April, the flamboyant tree, and the *matilishuat* with their bright red and delicate pink clusters of blossoms; tennis courts, a race track with a grandstand, and fields for football, baseball, basketball and volleyball combine to make this park a popular place for children and young people.

Moonlit nights afford a romantic setting under the shade trees for groups of youngsters with guitars and banjos, singing songs of long ago with a touch of nostalgia for colonial times.

Whether in the Campo de Marte, or on any of the well-paved streets of the city, the proportion of expensive automobiles is high; Salvadoreans are not addicted to walking, and it is only those who cannot afford even the cheapest cars, or the *cheles* (foreigners), who walk in the city.

A very pleasant drive along a good road is to a park near the crater of the San Salvador volcano, which looms over the city. Two roads lead to this *Parque del Boquerón* at an altitude of 6,333 feet, one by way of Santa Tecla, the other via the villages of Mejicanos and San Antonio Abad. Along the road to the Boquerón park are numerous estates with attractive homes, where San Salvador residents spend weekends or vacation time. Flowers from these gardens supply the city market. From an elevation on this road General Francisco Menéndez started a revolution against General Ezeta and was executed here August 1, 1890.

The *Finca Modelo,* a park on the southern side of town, is a bright, cool spot, near the *Escuela Normal de Varones.* The park called *La Ceiba,* a historic site by an ancient Ceiba tree, has experimental gardens on the Santa Tecla road.

From Planes de Renderos, where elegant residences have been built, there is a good road to Balboa Park with a magnificent view on all sides. From Los Planes there is also a road to the top of El Cerro de Chulul, an interesting place with two immense rocks marking what is known as *La Puerta del Diablo* (the Devil's doorway) with views of enormous valleys and mountain ranges.

The modern large park, *Parque de Oro,* is near the General Hospital, and is a delightfully well-kept place. Large shade trees, lawns, and a variety of flowers and plants contribute to make it a popular place for children; at one side below the road is a large dancing pavilion, also known as *El Parque de Los Niños.* It is flanked by large residences with gardens.

El Parque Centenario is near the *Jardín Infantil.* A nice drive is to *El Parque Atlacatl,* with extensive grounds, flowers, a forest of large trees, and modern laundry places *(lavaderos)* which provide water and conveniences for the women of this region; a *Sala Cuna* is annexed, where the small children of the laundresses get the full attention of trained nurses during the hours their mothers are busy earning their livings. A well-laid-out Zoological Garden is situated in the *Parque Modelo.*

In the heart of the town are the *Parque Bolívar* and *Plazoleta de Morazán.* The first-named lies before the Penitentiary Building. *Plaza Barrios* on the site of the colonial *Plaza de Armas* has been converted to *la Plaza de Carros,* where automobiles can conveniently be parked.

Plaza de los Diplomáticos is in the *Barrio de Candelaria* in front of the *Cuartel General de la Guardia Nacional* (National Guard). *Parque Venustiano Carranza* is named after General Venustiano Carranza, who gave the wireless tower to the country. Among other parks and squares are *El Parque Dueñas* or *Parque de la Independencia, Parque Cuzcatlán* with a very modern gymnasium, *Parque Bolívar,* and *Parque Belloso.*

MONUMENTS

El Salvador del Mundo is at the entrance to the city; the Saviour stands on an enormous pedestal with hand raised to bless the city. This statue was erected by popular subscription for the celebration of the Eucharistic Congress in 1942.

The *Avenida de la Independencia,* the street to the railroad station, has assorted statues of little merit. Life-size statues of Isabella and Fernando of Spain are at the entrance to the National Palace.

Gerardo Barrios has an artistic equestrian statue in the square of the same name.

In the *Parque Dueñas* or *de la Independencia* is a statue of General Juan J. Cañas, the author of the national anthem, and a bust of Felipe Soto, an outstanding musician. In the center is a column to commemorate the heroes of the Independence, erected on the first centenary of the cry of independence, 1911. Other monuments are those of Bartolomé de las Casas, Cristobal Colón, Miguel de Cervantes Saavedra (author of *Don Quijote*); the monument to the first Bishop of San Salvador, Dr. don Jorge Viteri y Ungo (consecrated in 1843) is in the vicinity of the Rosario Church. The statue of José Matías Delgado stands in the park of San José, in front of the San José Church.

A statue of Dr. Tomás Palomo in memory of the benefactor and surgeon is fittingly placed in front of the hospital building, as also is that of Dr. José Rosales, for whom the hospital is named. The Simón Bolívar monument is in the park of the same name.

At the entrance to the *Campo de Marte* a very artistic monument has the inscription: *Monumento eregido a la Memoria de los Mártires de la Patria, bajo la Administración del General Carlos Ezeta, 1893* (Monument dedicated to the memory of the martyrs of their country, under the administration of General Carlos Ezeta, 1893).

CHURCHES

The present edifices are for the most part temporary buildings wherein are worshiped relics and ancient images that have escaped disaster, not once but many times.

The Cathedral—It was a large, roomy, cool building. During the colonial period it was built on the site of the present El Rosario Church, facing the Plaza de Armas, having on the four sides of this park typical sidewalks with arcades, wherein elegant shops showed their best merchandise.

A great fire on August 8, 1951, totally destroyed the cathedral building and only at great hazard were some of the relics rescued from the flames. Fortunately among them was the venerated image of El Salvador del Mundo; not so the great Colonial organ by a Guatemalan artist. Now the plans are ready and the new building of solid concrete and steel will shortly replace the one that was destroyed and there will be an adequate cathedral to grace such a modern town as San Salvador.

Sunday mass was a fashionable gathering and all religious festivities were held in this building. Here was kept the famous *Salvador del Mundo* figure, which is taken out once a year on August 6 during the greatest festivity the city celebrates. This image was made from the wood of an orange tree that grew in the yard of the house of a devout sculptor, Silvestre García. This man asked permission from the *Real Audiencia* in Guatemala to carve the image in honor of *El Salvador del Mundo*, to whom he was devoted.

The *Fiestas Agostinas* (August feasts) are famous throughout Central America. Beginning in 1525, almost as soon as the city was established, a simple parade featuring the Royal Standard took place on August 6. However, the festivity developed rapidly during the eighteenth century, when the above-named García, a member of the Third Order of Franciscans, a sculptor and a painter, carved this image to fulfil a vow. Beginning in 1777, this good man endeavored to celebrate the feast with pomp and ceremony, privately defraying most of the expenses until his death in 1805. After that date, the municipality assumed the task and appointed sixteen stewardesses to have charge of the decorations for a period of six years. During the first year (1808), the celebrations were the same as formerly, but the next year one of the stewardesses, Dominga Mayorga, organized a pageant *(entrada)* with a float covered with wild flowers on which the famous *Salvador del Mundo* was carried. Every year after that a different allegorical float was made. The next step was a litter of wood and tinsel, with sundry decorations, on which the sacred image was carried around the *Plaza de Armas;* on one side the figure was unveiled: *El Descubrimiento.* Every year something has been added to the procession. Now the sacred image is hidden in a much decorated shell *(granada),* which at the corner of the *Parque Dueñas* is opened for *El Descubrimiento.* It is a breathtaking sight to watch the multitude kneel at a given signal as the sacred figure is revealed, and the procession then continues on its way back toward the Cathedral.

The present-day float is enormous and so tall that electric

wires must be cut to allow it to pass. Popular legend says that in the year that the figure by some mischance happens to fall, some catastrophe is in store for the country, specifically the president. The men who carry the float do it so as to fulfil a vow, and it is a penitence indeed on a hot day.

The colonial *entradas* are still celebrated by the *Capitana* or stewardess of each district of the city; according to her means she invites friends to participate, and to gather at her house to celebrate; the festive board groans under different kinds of sweetmeats, and everyone receives a present: little baskets of candies, artificial flowers, and the like, and then they go into the street to admire the decorated float that their district contributes toward the great procession.

Up and down the streets, Indians perform typical dances: *Historia, Los Moros, El Torito,* and others to the tune of the Indian fife and drum. Society disports itself at the clubs with dances and festivities. Military parades, races, and fireworks contribute toward the noise at this time of year. Repeatedly the attempt has been made to transfer the celebrations to the dry season instead of the August rainy season, but the custom is so entrenched that the people refused to take part in any festivities that did not take place in August on the day of the *Transfiguración del Señor.*

Nuestra Señora de la Merced—By a *Real Cédula,* in 1574, his Majesty the King ordered that convents and churches should be built. The Order of Mercedarios tried in 1593 to carry out this command, but did not succeed until 1623, when the church and convent were established. The bell tower was the scene of the first proclamation of independence, when Padre Matías Delgado in 1811 called on his people to free themselves from Spain. The convent and church subsequently were ruined, but part of this bell tower still remains as a sacred relic to the cause of independence.

El Rosario—This church is next to the Archbishop's Palace and is the setting for many San Salvador society weddings. Padre Matías Delgado is buried in this church.

Santo Domingo—For some reason the residents were opposed to the establishment of the Order of Santo Domingo, in the city. So the *Real Audiencia* from Guatemala sent three friars of this Order with Oidor Licenciado Tomás López to pacify the people. They built a church and convent in 1551 and filled it with artistic images and much silver. To this convent in 1790 was granted the privilege of guarding the documents belonging to the Order in this province. Unfortunately nothing remains of the buildings in the present city of San Salvador. It is worth while mentioning that the famous historian, Fray Francisco Jiménez, a Dominican, was prior of this convent in 1698.

San Francisco—In 1574, Fray Bernardino Perez was given a site whereon to build a church and convent of the Order of San Francisco de Padua, and he called it San Bernardino de Sena; later it was called San Antonio, and at the present time, San Francisco.

La Basílica—At a distance this building is reminiscent of some of the older European churches. It is disappointing when entering the building to find that it is a temporary construction and its imposing exterior nothing but a shell of seeming grandeur. It stands amid one of the pleasantest parts of the city, where beautiful houses with gardens denote their comfortable interiors and well-to-do owners.

San José—This church, though small, is one of the best constructed. The style is the oldest Spanish colonial architecture, wherein straight lines and an undecorated façade achieve a simplicity that is artistic. At one side is the Colegio de San José, a good school managed by priests.

La Candelaria—Situated in one of the poorer districts, it bears a sign showing the crest of the flood of the nearby Acelhuate River that drove many poor people from their homes and cut off the district of El Zapote from the rest of the city for almost a week.

Other Churches—In each district of the city, as well as in each of the new suburbs, churches have been built for the devout parishioners. Some are more like chapels, as is the one in the *Barrio de Santa Anita* donated by the De Sola family, who had the image of Santa Anita especially imported for this chapel. Another chapel is *El Espiritu Santo*.

The chapel of *El Buen Pastor* is part of the House of Correction for wayward girls. It is managed by the nuns; the girls are taught manual arts in which they excel, especially in fine sewing.

The Protestant Church—The Baptists have established a church where regular services are conducted by the resident pastor in the Avenida de Cuzcatlán. This denomination maintains a very large school presided over by a teacher from the U.S.A. The school building, in a cool spot on the San Jacinto Hill, is one of the handsomest and most fully earthquake-proof in the city.

CLUBS

El Casino at the corner of the Parque Barrios is the largest and best equipped club building in Central America, and is the gathering place of aristocratic Salvadoreans. Its swimming pool, restaurants, bowling alley, and billiard rooms are always well attended. The terrace on top of the building overlooks the city and distant hills, and affords a cool spot for an excellent dinner. A huge ballroom is the scene of superlative gaiety on specified dates, such as New Year's Eve, August 6, and September 15, besides smaller dances, equally well attended. It has a branch at Lake Ilopango.

The *International Club,* which recently has merged with El Casino, is an old institution and has a branch at the port of La Libertad.

El Círculo Militar was established and is conducted by army officers; this club is their gathering place. Several times during the year large dances take place. On December 12, the day of the Indian, this club has a fancy dress ball, at which everyone appears in Indian costume.

Besides the above named principal clubs, the *Rotarian Club* and *Lions Club* hold weekly meetings. Various Masonic lodges have regular meetings at their temple.

Sport Clubs

As with everything else, the capital city is the center for most of the sport activities. The beautiful *Country Club* has a spacious earthquake-proof building, with terraces from which one has a most soul-satisfying view of the setting sun, as it bathes the San Salvador volcano with roseate splendor to the delight of the many who are sitting at leisure on the terrace, or are playing golf or tennis. Large social balls take place at this club.

El Círculo Deportivo Salvadoreño (Club Deportivo International), has a comfortable and cool clubhouse, swimming pools, tennis courts, facilities for various other sports. At all times it is a gathering place for young sportsmen and girls from the city.

In both these above-mentioned clubs, sponsored travelers and visitors are extended the courtesy of the clubhouses and courses.

Club Hipico is popular and large crowds gather there on Sundays to watch the riders.

The Stadium on the southwest side of the city is the largest in Central America, and was erected for the Third Central American and Caribbean Olympic Games, scheduled for December, 1934, but transferred to 1935 because of a terrible hurricane, which devastated the city and surrounding country. Fourteen countries sent delegates to this event— the Stadium seats 35,000. The swimming pool is well attended every day of the week.

Swimming—Besides the swimming pools already mentioned, many private houses have pools. In *La Chacra,* situated in a ravine on the eastern side of the city, a large swimming pool with shady trees, up-to-date showers and dressing rooms, restaurant, and every convenience for the sportsman is available. The waters of the Acelhuate are used for this pool, and a magic transformation has been wrought; formerly the black waters of the city polluted this river, and are now drained through huge concrete pipes to faraway places.

Archives, Public Library, and David Joaquin Guzmán Museum

As a result of the many seismic disturbances, few of the old documents have survived. A few territorial grants and titles dating from the colonial era are gathered in the *Departamento de Historia* annexed to the National Museum.

The Museum was established under the administration of Dr. Rafael Zaldívar, president of the Republic in 1883, and founded by the eminent botanist, David Joaquin Guzmán. Its best exhibits are archaeological specimens found in different parts of the country. Good polychrome vessels and a large stone *Chacmool* were discovered near Ahuachapán. This type of figure seems to be associated with the Nahuatl period. There are other interesting pre-Columbian objects, which are now being carefully classified. Zoological, mineralogical, and paleontological exhibits are part of the museum.

The Public Library has a worthwhile collection of Latin-American works. Its outstanding treasures are, of course, the incunabula of which it possesses several tomes.

Other Places of Interest

Theaters—When fire destroyed the National Theater in 1910, the present building was erected. It has an imposing exterior, but the interior is not at all adequate for a city of the size and rank of San Salvador; it is generally used as a movie house. All movie theaters are under the direct monopoly of the government.

El Ateneo—This is a historical and literary society, with a quarterly bulletin, *El Ateneo*. Many brilliant lecturers and distinguished scientists have spoken before this group. Its members are much interested in furthering the native arts and crafts in the various regions of the country, and in unifying them.

Forts. The city is well garrisoned. Some of the forts that watch over the city are of unique architecture, though of no particular period. In the heart of town is the artillery garrison, which has always taken an active part in every revolt. The formidable *Cuartel de El Zapote* is situated on the hill of the same name overlooking the city, on the south side.

The Cemetery—On the western side of the city is the last resting place of many well-known men such as Morazán. It is a well-kept place and has many artistic statues in addition to monuments on every grave. It is well worth visiting on November 1 and 2, when the graves are superbly decorated with flowers—both natural and artificial.

Markets—Four principal markets hum with activity, and are the scene of teeming humanity in the early hours of the morning. Produce from the outlying districts arrives on the shoulders and backs of men and women: eggs and fowl in large baskets on the heads of the picturesque Panchimalco Indians, tropical vegetables and fruit from farms on the slopes of the volcanoes and hills near the city, luscious fresh fruit such as pineapples, pawpaws, mangoes, jícaras, coyoles, sincuyas, and many others not known to any northern palate, but delicious when in season. Meat hangs in protected stalls, breads of all kinds are temptingly displayed, sweetmeats are of the most delectable colors and shapes and entice youngsters to buy. All in all, everything that a big city desires is fresh every day.

In the booths on the sides are displayed baskets, gourds, clay figures, and the like, scrambled together with shoes, articles of clothing, cheap jewelry, and other odds and ends. Outside the main market, booths display Indian and non-Indian crafts: rope, henequen articles, wooden stirrups and horse-gear, ceramics from Paleca and Aculhuaca, tinware, corn husk dolls, and everything typical of this country.

The overflow of the markets spreads to the four sides of the adjacent streets; a good bargain may be achieved outside as well as inside. Bargaining is the high spot of marketing, and nobody, neither merchant nor buyer, is satisfied if even a carrot has not been bargained for, and perhaps reduced a cent in the transaction.

One of the markets that is well stocked with meat has primitive charcoal stoves that cook Salvadorean dishes for the hungry out-of-town people. *El Emporio* is the market used exclusively for flowers. Quantities and endless varieties of flowers come to this market very early—orchids when in season, Easter lilies, roses, and other semitropical and tropical flowers. Gardenias are the most common flower and the strong perfume from large baskets filled with them pervades the whole building. It is not alone the natural flowers that make this market a bright and satisfying spot, but everywhere quantities of artificial flowers, the brighter the better, are mixed with the fresh blooms, as artificial flowers are popular, and the people are adept at their manufacture.

Public Buildings—The architecture of the public buildings is slowly changing. The temporary buildings are being replaced, and the Post Office, the University with its other buildings on the *Avenida Universitaria,* the modern building of *El Ministerio de Trabajo,* are brilliant examples of the new style. The new university section of the city has well-built walls, with adequate light and ventilation for a warm climate. The University is famous for its courses, and many prominent individuals have graduated from it.

The *President's Palace* on the *Cerro de El Zapote* is an imposing building.

El Palacio de Comunicaciones, Palacio Nacional de Comunicaciones Eléctricas. The telegraph, telephone, radio, and cable are all housed in this building in the center of the town.

The *National Palace (Palacio Nacional)*, built on the four sides of a square around a center garden, has wide staircases and imposing rooms; in it the different ministeries of the government have their offices. The original building was destroyed by fire on November 19, 1889.

The *National Police Palace* also houses the immigration offices. The very modern *Airport* outside the city is at the Ilopango field.

The *Military School* building is on the Santa Tecla road; besides those already mentioned there are several under construction.

Symbols of San Salvador—The City of San Salvador has a special flag and coat of arms, conferred on November 5, 1943, by the Municipality of the City. One quarter of the coat of arms symbolizes the bell that was rung from the Church of La Merced by Padre Delgado. In another quarter there is an emerald necklace, symbol of Indian Cuzcatlán. In the other two quarters are the colors of the national flag. Circling the symbols are the dates 1525, the year the town was established; 1811, the famous first cry of independence; and 1821, when independence became a reality. The flag has seven horizontal stripes, blue and white, with a red square in the upper left corner, wherein the coat of arms of the city is placed.

The words and music of the anthem are a song of praise to the city and its people, who have bravely faced calamities with valor, courage, and conquering spirit. The words are by Carlos Bustamante and the music by C. de Jesús Alas.

Villages near the City

Several villages within walking or driving distance near the city are interesting during their feast days; distances are from San Salvador.

Apopa: Distance: 16 km north. Population: 2,568. Feast: Santa Catarina, Nov. 22-25.

Good roads, lush coffee region, large sugar mill. Good ceramics. Name means "Smoking water" or "Place of the mists."

Ayutuxtepeque: D: 6 km northwest. P: 470. F: San Sebastián, last Sunday in October and last Sunday in January with three days of celebrations.

Colonial church with a few art treasures; valuable *La Virgen del Socorro* might be the work of a Mexican artist; typical painted eyebrows and lashes of Mexican artists. Name means "Place of the armadillo" (turtle rabbit). Very old village, mentioned in 1770 as part of the jurisdiction of Mexicanos.

Cuzcatancingo: D: 4 km northwest. P: 1,579. F: Virgen de Concepción, Dec. 7-9.

Rivalry exists between the people from this village and those of San Antonio Abad because of the former's devotion to San Antonio Abad, whose feast starts in this village and continues in the latter. The San Antonio people call these *Los del Valle* (from the valley); good dances with typical music at feasts. Name means in Pipil "The place of the small Cuzcatlán."

Ilopango: D: 8 km east. P: 2,950. F: San Cristobal, Nov. 12-16.

Name Ilopango or Xilopango means "In the place of the goddess of the corn spikes." Good road. Railroad station, near the International Airport.

Mejicanos: D: 4 km north. P: 7,295. F: Virgen del Tránsito, Aug. 15-16.

Founded by the Mexican Indians of Pedro de Alvarado's army. Attractive church. During feasts, typical dances take place reminiscent of the colonial period. Near La Rábida colony, where beautiful archaeological pieces have been found when digging for foundations for houses and gardens. The parochial church in 1814 was the meeting place for the individuals working for independence from Spain.

Nueva San Salvador or **Santa Tecla:** D: 12 km west. P: 18,604. F: La Pascua de Navidad, Dec. 19-25.

Though a distinct entity it is considered part of the city as the people do all their shopping and marketing here. The feast is well attended by people from San Salvador. City society drives up here in the afternoons for their outing along the paved road that connects the two places.

Santa Tecla is the capital of the department of La Libertad (population 25,000). Situated on the south slope of the San Salvador or Quezaltepeque volcano, it was established in 1854 as the capital of the Republic when San Salvador was destroyed by earthquakes. It was legally declared the capital from February 3, 1855, until 1859, when the authorities of the Republic returned to the site of San Salvador. Five kilometers to the south on the highway to La Libertad are clear springs and a small river, Ayagualo, with good bathing houses.

Panchimalco: D: 16 km south. P: 2,950. F: Santa Cruz de Roma, Sept. 13-16.

On good road. Name means "Place of flags and coat of arms" or "Fortified place." Population almost all of Nahoa origin. Indians known as *Panchitas* established village in 1611 on top of high hill with good scenery across valleys and mountains. At back of village, *El Chulo*. Colonial baroque church at the highest point of village. Indian huts scattered in the underbrush. Large amatle tree by church is the center of village life. The feast is well attended for its procession, typical sales, sports with greased pole, and racing. The villagers speak the Nahuatl language. Handmade simple ceramics of good lines. Twelve kilometers southeast is interesting hamlet, Amayo; name derived from *amolli,* a tree whose fruit is used instead of soap *(jaboncillo* or *pacum).*

San Antonio Abad: D: 6 mi. northwest. F: San Antonio Abad, Jan. 16-18.

Small village on slope of **San Salvador** volcano. Sleepy village awakens for the feast with typical masked dances, ringing of church bells; religious procession headed by a large float, preceded by small girls in blue dresses with silver ribbons and many flowers, and carrying long reeds. Every time the procession stops along the way, the children cry copiously until the float is lifted. This custom is a vow that mothers of the children have made to the Almighty, so that He will shower blessings on them for the coming year. The Figure on the float is uncovered before the kneeling multitude on its way back to the church.

San Marcos: D: 5 km southeast. P: 2,540, rural and urban. F: San Marcos, Apr. 24-26; El Tránsito, Aug. 14-16.

Ancient village on south slope of San Jacinto Hill named by Spaniards in 1770.

Santiago Texacuangos: D: 12 km east. P: 5,000, rural and urban. F: Señor Santiago, Jul. 24-25; San Mateo, Sept. 20-21.

Very old Indian village, part of Santo Tomás. Pipil name *Texacuangos* means "High stone valley."

Soyapango: D: 4 km east. P: 3,000. F: Virgen del Rosario, Oct. 5-12.

Established 1717. Paved road. Region where cereals and sugarcane grow. Pipil name means "Valley of the corozo palm."

A. Paleca: D: 5 km northeast. F: San Miguel Arcángel, Sept. 26-29.

Typical Indian dances during feasts. Famous for its ceramics. Name means "Place of the red clay."

B. Aculhuaca: D: 4 km northeast. F: Santiago, Jul. 26.

Church in classic colonial style. Crafts and produce from gardens sold on city markets. Name means "Place of the strong men" or "Place of the Aculhua Indians."

C. San Sebastián Texincal: D: 4 km northeast. F: San Sebastián, Jan. 17-20.

Typical processions and Indian dances. Church, with double Ionic columns, has good altars and six good ancient paintings. Name means "stone houses."

The villages **A, B,** and **C** named above were united in 1935 as **Villa Delgado,** forming one political entity with 13,504 inhabitants. Named in honor of the priest, José Matías Delgado.

XX

TOWNS AND VILLAGES

IT IS impossible to list completely all the towns and villages in the country. Those of the greatest interest and having the largest populations have been selected.

The capital of each department is joined to the capital of the country by good highways. Other villages have either roads or trails joining them with the capital of the department in which they are situated. Distances shown are from the capital of the department unless otherwise specified.

Better to understand the country, I have quoted from the article of Jorge Ladé y Larín in *Recopilación de Leyes Relativas a la Historia de los Municipios de El Salvador*. Geographically the country is divided in three zones. Each zone is integrated by a certain number of departments: three correspond to the west, seven to the center, and four to the east. Administratively each department is divided into districts, each district into *municipios*, and each *municipio* into *cantones*.

Data for the principal town and village populations are taken in part from an article by Jorge Ladé y Larín in *El Diario de Hoy*, June 9, 1952.

Acajutla or **Acaxutla**, Sonsonate. E: sea level. P: 1,500. From Sonsonate 19 km southwest.

Name means "Place of the turtle and canes." One of the principal ports on the Pacific Ocean. Founded by Pedro de Alvarado on his trip to Peru in 1534. Open roadstead. Warm climate. Good swimming beach. Several times destroyed by fire but reconstructed. Connected with the capital, Santa

Ana, and other coffee-producing districts by railroad (Salvador Railroad Company). Near this port are the beaches of Los Cóbanos.

> **Ahuachapán,** capital of department of same name. E: 820 m. P: 10,426. From San Salvador 101 km west. F: Dulce Nombre de Jesús on movable date and El Tránsito, Aug. 15.

Name means "Town of the oak houses." Good roads and railroad connection. Hot springs from the falls of Malacatiupán with bath houses, besides other hot springs and bathing places nearby. Interesting small lake, El Llano del Espino. Favorite spot for picnics at the falls of Atehuezian, which supply the city's electric light and power. The falls are 150 feet high, situated four kilometers west of the town; eight kilometers east is the river "Cashal" with public bathing houses. The name *Ahuachapán* is derived from Uetzi-Apan. Despite the Indian population, this place attracted many Spaniards and *mestizos,* who named it "Nuestra Señora de la Asunción Ahuachapán." The Hills of Apaneca (flower culture) are sixteen kilometers east. A favorite place for excursions is San Lorenzo, situated on the River Paz; also the Laguna del Lano, with good fishing.

> **Alegría,** Usulután. E: 1,200 m. P: 2,000. From Usulután 24 km north-northwest. F: San Pedro, Jun. 29; San Miguel, Sept. 29; "La del Niño," Jan. 1.

Occupied by Lenca Indians and known as Tecapa, name changed to Alegría in 1891 in honor of the educator Miguel José Alegría. Good roads to principal places. Region for coffee, cattle ranches, and large coffee mills. Name *Tecapa* means "Lagoon of stone" or "In the valley on the hill"; two kilometers from village are hot springs located in a hollow 300 meters in diameter. The noise of the boiling water is heard at least two miles distant. Hot springs in crater of Tecapa volcano two kilometers from town is a

popular bathing place. On the shores sulphur and white clay
are abundant.

Anamoros, La Unión. P: 1,000. From La Unión 16 km north.
F: of the Virgin, Aug. 14-15. Fair: Santa Teresa, Oct. 13-16.

Nearby gold and silver mine, Carmelo Providencia. On
pre-Columbian site of Lenca Indians, near Anamorós River.
Established in 1737.

Antiguo Cuzcatlán, La Libertad. P: 550. From Santa Tecla 4
km. southeast. F: Dec. 26-28.

Mentioned as being the site in 1054 of the pre-Columbian
headquarters of the *cacicazco* of Cuzcatlán.

Apaneca, or **Apanehecatl,** Ahuachapán. E: 1,600 m. P: 2,046.
F: San Andrés, Nov. 27-30.

Indian name means "River of wind," very correctly because of high winds blowing from nearby Lagunita and
Cumbre volcanoes. Another derivation of name indicates a
Nahoa descent of the inhabitants: "Home of the Apanecas."
It is interesting that an aboriginal manuscript, *Codex Borgia,*
of the Mexicans mentions an immigration captained by three
chiefs, one named Apaneca, which might well have been the
origin of the name of the village.

Apastepeque, San Vicente. E: 640 m. P: 2,920. From San
Vicente 4 km north. F: Santiago, Jul. 19-25; San Sebastián,
Jan. 20; Santa Rita, May 22.

Good roads, region of sugarcane and cereals, and large
estates. Name means "Hill of the *apastes*" (large open clay
pots). Northeast of town is a lagoon, Laguna Viva, to dis-
tinguish it from its neighbor, Laguna Ciega. The first-named
is large, with beautiful scenery, many fish and waterfowl. It
is one kilometer north of the Pan American Highway. The

second is covered with floating vegetation; during the rainy months of September and October quantities of fish are caught between the plants.

Arcatao, Chalatenango. P: 1,304. From Chalatenango 32 km northeast. F: Candelaria, Feb. 1-3.

Ancient pre-Columbian Lenca site. Fertile region for coffee, indigo, cereals, sweet potatoes, and yam beans. Through town runs River Guayampopo. Half a kilometer distant is La Sirena pool, in a basin of rock with falls of eight-meter height, a favorite bathing place.

Armenia (San Silvestre), Sonsonate. P: 6,500. From Sonsonate 28 km east. F: San Silvestre, Dec. 31.

Indian name means "The great oratory on the road." Rich agricultural region and cattle ranches. Nearby is Los Lagartos River, whose Indian *Pipil* name was *Guaymuco,* "Frog oratory."

Ataco, Ahuachapán. P: 3,200. From Ahuachapán 8 km south. F: La Virgen de Concepción, Dec. 8-16; San Lucas, Oct. 16-18; San José, Mar. 17-19.

An ancient establishment on *Pipil* site. Site at the top of the hill *La Empalizada* or *Ataco.* Cool climate. Name means "Place of the high water springs."

Atiquizaya, Ahuachapán. E: 623 m. P: 5,823. From Ahuachapán 16 km northeast. Fair: Dec. 5-8.

Town established in 1662. Very rich agricultural region: coffee, cereals, sugarcane, vanilla, rubber and henequen. Indian word means "Where the raingod is" or "Place of the springs." (Nearby are 27 springs.)

Berlin, Usulután. E: 900 m. P: 4,500. From Usulután 40 km northwest. F: San José, Mar. 15-20.

An important town in the midst of coffee regions and valuable estates, on the slopes of Tecapa volcano. Established 1885.

Cacaopera, Morazán. P: 1,740. From San Francisco 12 km northeast. F: Virgen del Tránsito, Aug. 6-10; New Year feast, Jan. 1; La Cruz, May 2-3.

Indian name means "Place of the cacao." The inhabitants make rope saddlebags and other fiber merchandise from the maguey plant, and other textile fibers that they sell on the San Miguel market.

California, Usulután. P: 1,063. From Usulután 2 km. F: Niño Jesús, Dec. 22-25.

Good roads, valuable coffee estates. Founded in 1897.

Cancasque, Chalatenango. P: 779. From Chalatenango 20 km southeast. F: San José, Mar. 18-19.

Important mining region, gold and silver. Good water supply from Agua Fría River, having a spectacular waterfall at least 12 yards high.

Candelaria, Cuzcatlán. P: 1,000. From Cojutepeque 8 km southwest. F: Dulce Nombre de María, Nov. 14-15.

Region for coffee, cereals, and manufacture of black sugar (*panela*). Established in 1872.

Candelaria de la Frontera, Santa Ana. P: 1,245. From Santa Ana 24 km northwest. F: Candelaria, Jan. 31 to Feb. 4.

East-northeast of village is Cacalotepeque Hill (meaning "hill of the crow"). Place of entry into the country from the Republic of Guatemala; luggage and passports are examined here.

Chalatenango, Chalatenango. E: 506 m. P: 4,200. From San
Salvador 78 km northeast. F: Pascua de Navidad, Dec. 20-
25. Fair: Feria de los Santos, Oct. 21-Nov. 5; San Juan
Bautista, Jun. 24, with processions.

Highway to Honduras north of this town. Pre-Columbian
site of Lencas and later populated by Pipil Indians. Spaniards established this place in 1791 by order of Baron
Garardalet, General Governor of the Kingdom of Guatemala,
so that indigo cultivations should be intensified. Region of
cattle ranches, sheep, and agricultural produce: corn, beans,
sugar, coffee, fiber plants, plantains.

Chalchuapa, Santa Ana. E: 639 m. P: 9,980. From Santa Ana
16 km southwest. F: Santiago, Jul. 17-21. Railroad station.

Former name, Chalchigüit, means "River of the swamps"
or "River of jadeites." General Justo Rufino Barrios, president of Guatemala, was killed near this place in a battle
in 1885. Old colonial establishment, as well as a pre-Columbian site. Some of the walls of the houses have shards incrusted therein. River Pampe south of town, also large lava
bed.

Colonial church is interesting because of its style: a com-
bination of primitive Spanish colonial, severe lines, combined with Indian characteristics; the Spaniards directed the
construction, but the Indians worked so well that the Indian
artist molded some of his personality into the construction.

On west side of cemetery are located interesting ruins:
Teocalli of Tazumal, where the so-called "Virgin of Tazumal" was found. Polychrome and simple black pottery have
been found in these ruins. The ruins of Pampe are toward
the north in the valley of that river. It is stated that in the
eleventh century all this region was inhabited by Lenca
Indians. These were later ousted by Pokomanes, who in turn
were superseded by migrations of Nahuatl or Pipiles from
the north. A prehistoric population existed near here called

Cuscashapá, destroyed by the eruption of a volcano, where now is the Laguna Chalchuapa.

Chiltiupan, La Libertad. P: 2,908. From Santa Tecla 56 km southwest. Fair: San Marcos, Apr. 25; Santo Domingo, Aug. 4.

Established in 1553. Situated in a hilly region on the mountain slope of the coastal mountains, region of cattle ranches and agriculture. Name means "Red sanctuary."

Chilanga, Morazán. P: 1,150. From San Francisco 4 km north. F: María Magdalena, Jul. 19-22; María Exaltación, Sept. 13-14; Virgen de Concepción, Dec. 6-8.

A prehistoric Lenca site. Region of henequen and palm leaf hat crafts. Name means "In the red reeds."

Chinameca, San Miguel. E: 600 m. P: 6,450. From San Miguel 24 km west. F: three fairs and fiestas: San Juan, Jun. 22-24; Fiestas Agostinas, Aug. 1-8; Guadalupe, Dec. 8-14.

Good agricultural region: indigo, tobacco, sugar cane, cereals. Indian original name was *Yusique,* meaning "Place of the pines." The present name means "Place of *Chinamas*" or "Place of *rancherias.*" In 1951 Chinameca was destroyed. The colonial church was in ruins, a great loss, as it was one of the few outstanding monuments of that period.

Chirilagua, San Miguel. P: 2,400. From San Miguel 50 km south. F: Virgen de Guadalupe, Dec. 8-13.

Industrial crafts center: palm leaf hats, reed mats, rope, and other fiber articles. Eighteen kilometers east of the hot springs, El Borbollon; fourteen kilometers north to scenic mountain Buenavista. Name means "The three stars."

Cuidad Barrios, San Miguel. P: 2,270. D: 48 km north-north-west of San Miguel. F: Señor de Roma, Jan. 21-22; San Pedro, Jun. 28-29. Fair, Feb. 12-16.

Indian name, *Cacahuatique,* means "Cacao plantations," established by Royal Grant in 1711. The name was changed from Cacahuatique to Ciudad Barrios in 1913, in honor of General Gerardo Barrios, who was born here and in his youth was Municipal Secretary. The town is situated on the west slope of the Cacaguatique volcano.

Coatepeque (San Pedro), Santa Ana. E: 690 m. P: 2,200. From Santa Ana 16 km southeast. F: San Pedro, Jun. 27-30; Fair, 2-3 Friday of Lent.

Site of battle in 1863 between troops under General Gerardo Barrios against Guatemalan troops led by President General Rafael Carrera, who was defeated. Near scenic Lake Coatepeque. Church is rather on the neoclassic style with Doric columns, probably of the eighteenth century. Name means "Hill or place of the snakes." The church has a famous image of Jesús de los Milagros in natural size, supposedly the work of the Guatemalan artist Quirio Cataño. A famous pilgrimage and fair was instituted in 1794, called *Romería de Jesús de los Milagros o Feria de los Viernes.*

Cojutepeque, Cuzcatlán. E: 2,920 ft. P: 10,252. From San Salvador 40 km east. F: San Juan, June 15-30; Patron Saint San Sebastián and Concepción, Jan. 12-21.

Railroad station and good roads to capital. In Nahuatl the name means "On the enchanted hill." Situated on the north slope of Cerro de las Pavas, famous for its scenic beauty and a favorite place for picnics, having a pavilion on the top. In the background is a view of Chachacaste Hill, famous because of the numerous battles fought there. The town has a pretty park named after Rafael Cabrera, a famous poet who was born here. Town was established before 1571.

The best time to visit it is during the August cattle fair. It has several historical buildings such as *Casa Consistorial,* where the Federal Government of Central America had its seat during the Union. Likewise when the Salvadorean Government headed by Don Rafael Campo took refuge from the destruction by earthquakes of the capital, this building became the government headquarters. In the dome of the San Sebastian church the famous Reloj de Abderramán III kept perfect time from 1839 to 1887.

Colon, La Libertad. P: 900. From Santa Tecla 6 km west. F: El Señor de Esquipulas, Jan. 13-15, established in 1886.

Agricultural region: corn, cereals, and cattle ranches. Built on the site of the old village of Guarumal. Mentioned because it is on the road to Lake Coatepeque.

Comacaran, San Miguel. P: 2,000. From San Miguel 16 km northeast. F: San Sebastian, Jan. 19-21.

Name means "Hill of the Peppers," mentioned in history as in 1770 annexed to the Parish of Ereguayquín. Region of silver and gold mines.

Comazahua, La Libertad. E: 1,150 m. P: 1,169. From Santa Tecla 16 km southwest. F: San Mateo, Sept. 27.

On the mountain range. Nearby is river of same name. Important coffee district, corn, beans, rice, and potatoes. Built on pre-Columbian Pipil site; six kilometers south is high rock, El Kepi Salvadoreño (The Salvadorean cap), also called *Piedra de Santiago* or *Piedra Herrada* by the sailors cruising this coast, because of its shape and the curious figures cut into the rock. Steps have been cut so that visitors may ascend to the top to view the Pacific Ocean and most of the Salvadorean territory.

Conchagua, La Unión. E: 900 m. P: 2,325. From La Unión 4 km south-southwest.

Founded by refugees from the Island of Conchagüita who fled from British pirate persecution, and live at various altitudes up and down the slopes of the volcano of the same name. Established in 1682.

Concepción Quezaltepeque, Chalatenango. P: 1,959. From Chalatenango 11 km northwest. F: Concepción, Dec. 7-8.

Region of indigo and maguey. Near the village there is a hill of pink earth, used for coloring crafts; also a hill having a ridged peak. Old Indian village site. Name means "Hill of the quetzal bird."

Corinto, Morazán. P: 1,400. From San Francisco 24 km northeast. F: Día de los Reyes, Jan. 6; San Pedro and San Pablo, Jun. 29.

Region of cereals, established in 1882.

El Carmen, Cuzcatlán. P: 3,114. From Cojutepeque 2 km east. F: El Carmen, Jul. 16.

Good road and railroad station; railroad tunnel goes through *Cerro Partido* (Divided rock).

El Carmen, La Unión. P: 3,770. From La Unión 21 km west. F: El Carmen, Jul. 16.

Fertile valley watered by the River Los Almendros. Established in 1874.

El Paisnal, San Salvador. P: 1,150. From San Salvador, 48 km north northeast. F: Fair of San José, Mar. 16-20.

Northwest eight kilometers is Cinatepeque, hill of scenic beauty.

El Rosario. Four different villages go by the name of **El Rosario: El Rosario, la Paz.** P: 1,275. From Zacatecoluca 24 km west. F: Virgen del Rosario, Oct. 18-19.

Region of forests with variety of construction and furniture woods. Northwest of village there is a tunnel ten meters long, three meters high, and four meters wide, providing a natural passage from one side to the other of the hill.

Rosario de Mora, jurisdiction of Panchimalco, established 1894.

El Rosario, jurisdiction of Cojutepeque, established 1872.

El Rosario, jurisdiction of San Pedro Mazahuat, established 1847.

El Tránsito, San Miguel. P: 2,000. From San Miguel 32 km F: El Tránsito, Aug. 1-15; San José, Mar. 17-19.

Region for tobacco and cereals, cattle ranches. Established 1914.

Erreguayquin, Usulután. P: 2,500. From Usulután 7 km northeast. F: de Jesús, Jan. 13-15; San Benito, May 14-15.

Indian and *ladino* village. The parish church is a well-preserved colonial relic. On the highway from Usulután to San Miguel. Suffered greatly by pirate incursions in 1683. Name means "Village of the falcons."

Guatejiagua, Morazán. P: 3,320. From San Francisco 16 km southwest. F: Santiago Apóstol, Jul. 23-25; San Sebastián, Jan. 18-20; San José, Mar. 18-19; Pascua de Navidad, Dec. 24-25.

Modern place on ancient site of pre-Columbian village.

Guayabal, Cuzcatlán. P: 1,600. From Cojutepeque 32 km northwest. F: Patron Saint San José, Mar. 18-20. Fair: Jesús del Rescate, Jan. 15 to Feb. 2.

To the east is Agua Caliente, a river with good thermal springs.

Guazapa, San Salvador. P: 1,990. From San Salvador 28 km north. F: San Miguel Arcángel, Sept. 28-29.

Pre-Columbian site. Name means "Resounding rock" or "River of the *guace* birds" (who announce the beginning and end of the rainy season; in other places called *azacuanes*).

Huizucar, La Libertad. P: 1,500. From Santa Tecla 16 km southeast. F: San Miguel Arcángel, Sept. 29; Magdalena, Jun. 22.

Indian Pipil name means "Place on the road of the thorns." Probably a pre-Columbian village near the River Amaquilco or Las Lajas; four kilometers west is *Cerro del Caballero* (Hill of the gentlemen), with a queer figure of a man holding some leaves and the letter *K* inscribed thereon. Region of good coffee and cereal plantations. Near village is a cool swimming pool in the River Huiza. Name means "Where man was born," or, in other words, "The Indian paradise."

Ilobasco, Cabañas. P: 3,380. From Sensuntepeque 38 km west. F: Los Desamparados, 3d Sunday in May; San Miguel, Sept. 28-29; Concepción, Dec. 7-8.

Famous for its ceramics. Nearby Los Cerritos Hill is a popular place for outings. Four kilometers west is Los Frailes of Copinol River. Region for indigo, cereals, and cattle ranches.

Legend states that the image of San Miguel, Patron Saint of the village, disappeared from Sitio Viejo, six kilometers northwest of present village. Twice it was found and disappeared again and finally was found on the trunk of a tree at a site whereon the present *parroquia* was built, so the parish priest convinced his Indian parishioners to move to this modern site in 1859.

Ishuatan (Santa Isabel Ixhuatán), Sonsonate. P: 1,312. From Sonsonate 38 km southeast. F: Santo Niño de Atoche, Feb. 13-16; Santa Isabel, Nov. 20-30.

Nearby river is the Apancoyo. Region for coffee, cereals, and balsam, and cattle ranches. Name means "Place of earthquakes."

Izalco, Sonsonate. P: 7,588. From Sonsonate 8 km northeast. F: Ascension, Aug. 9-15; Concepción, Dec. 1-10; Virgen de los Remedios, Dec. 1-20; San Juan Bautista, Jun. 18-24; Christmas Eve, Dec. 24.

Izalco means "Place of the obsidian houses." Itzcoatlco means "On or over the obsidian serpent."

Twin villages, Dolores Izalco and Asunción Izalco, the latter of Indians only, known as Pueblo de Abajo. His Majesty ordered these villages to be divided; it was an important center for cacao production, and an important site in the pre-Columbian era. Philip II granted this village the title of "Villa" in 1580. It received that of "Ciudad" in 1869. Situated on the lower slope of Izalco Volcano, it commands a gorgeous view of the Balsam Coast. The Indian village is typical, with huts hidden in the dense foliage. The Indians still speak Nahuatl or Pipil. Large crosses on principal streets mark the celebrations for the *Fiesta de la Cruz.* The most important and principal place of worship is *La Cruz Galante.*

A brook, dry in summer and turbulent in the rainy season, divides the village. It is called *Quebrada de los Olotes,* because after the seed grain has been prepared for the crop, the dry corncobs are thrown into this small ravine. On one side of this place a small hill shaded by a towering tamarind tree is called *Cuesta de la Muerte;* it is near the place where, legend states, "Pedro de Alvarado on his horse came this way, and spied a pretty Indian maid. The girl was frightened and ran to hide in the bush." Alvarado followed. The ravine was a torrent of water and the girl in terror threw herself into it. Alvarado leaped to her rescue but could not find her. The imprint of his foot and that of his horse have remained for all time on the largest stone of the ravine, which is known as *La Piedra de Alvarado.*

The village still has its own Indian chief and Indian Court of Justice to judge its own people. A fairly large parochial church is in the seventeenth-century colonial style. The ruined church on the other side of the village was built by the Spaniards in the sixteenth century; the ruins show the usual thick walls and solid construction. The cupola and part of the former temple must have been well decorated, to judge by the remains. The oratory is preserved; placed in a special niche on the crest of the hill is the image of the Virgen de la Concepción. Flowers and pine surround this sacred spot.

The massive church bell was brought by the Spaniards; the most famous is the bronze bell which bears this inscription: *María Asunción me llaman, 100 quintales peso, el que no lo creyere, que me levante el peso* (My name is María Asunción, I weigh 100 quintals, he who doubts it, should lift me to prove it). This bell was cast in 1580 in Sevilla and donated to the village by His Gracious Majesty Charles V, King of Spain. The legend says that the bell was buried for many years under the ruins of the old church, and is charmed. Only the pure hands of maidens may touch it. This Lady Bell is considered as the sovereign mother of the village inhabitants, and the women have woven their finest scarves for it.

Los Chichimecos is danced in the village of Izalco on the day of *Las Mercedes;* small children take a prominent part in this strictly Christian popular performance.

Half a mile east from Izalco are medicinal sulphurous

baths springing directly from the volcano, called *Atecozol,* meaning "Water in stone cradles." On an occasion when lava flow from the volcano Izalco hastened down to the village, prayers and offerings stopped the menace on the outskirts of town, where now is erected a statue to Our Saviour. The feast of San Juan is celebrated by horsemen who try to cut off the heads of four cocks which are hung on a pole. When finished, they try to unseat one another to the music of fife and drum.

The produce from this region is marketed in the nearby town of Sonsonate, with which it is connected by an antiquated mule tramway.

Many of the Indians rebelled in 1932; it was supposedly a communist upheaval, but in reality constituted a rebellion of Indians against the whites. The Indians hid in the mountains and concealed their treasures under the floors of their huts. Many were killed, and the survivors meekly returned, much subdued.

Jayaque, La Libertad. E: 800 m. P: 2,848. From Santa Tecla 28 km west-southwest. F: San Sebastian, Jan. 17-20; San Cristóbal, Jul. 18-25; and Holy Week.

On the northern slopes of the coastal mountain chain. Original name Xayacat, meaning "Hill of the masked men." Rich coffee and cattle region. Present site established in 1700, because the first site was prone to epidemics and plagues.

Jiquilisco, Usulután. E: 220 m. P: 5,837. From Usulután 20 km southwest. F: Fair, El Tránsito, Aug. 15-20.

Region of forests with splendid woods. Indian name probably derived because the town faces the azure waters of the Jiquilisco Bay ("facing the turquoise"), or it might be "The indigo cultivators," as this region is a rich place for indigo, also called *jiquilite.*

Jocoaitique, Morazán. P: 3,000. From San Francisco 36 km north. F: Virgen de la Merced, Sept. 7-8; Los Reyes, Jan. 5-6; and San Jose, Mar. 18-19.

Situated on stony ground on right margin of Agua Caliente brook. A fire destroyed in 1784 all municipal archives, which probably had records of the old establishment. Name means "Hill of the five fires."

Jocoro, Morazán. P: 6,000. From San Francisco 16 km southeast. F: Candelaria, Feb. 1-2; Virgen de la Merced, Sept. 7-8; and María Auxiliadora, May 24.

Gold and silver mines, also region for indigo, sugarcane and cereals. On the plains near village the Nicaraguan and Honduran forces under General Morazán vanquished in 1832 the Salvadorean army under General Gregorio Villaseñor.

Juayua, Sonsonate. P: 3,320. From Sonsonate 16 km northnorthwest. F: El Señor de Juayua, Jan. 8-18; Santa Lucía, Dec. 8-14.

Good climate, old establishment, large-scale coffee plantations and coffee mills. Northwest are Los Naranjos Hills where the Ceniza River has its springs. Name means either "Place of red orchids" or "Place of the sour waters," because of the proximity of the alkaline springs of the River Las Calderas.

Jucuapa, Usulután. P: 6,122. From Usulután 28 km northeast. F: San Simón, Oct. 25-30; Concepción, Dec. 7-8.

Good roads. Rich coffee region. Situated at the foot of the Jucuapa volcano. Totally destroyed May 7-8, 1951. Inhabitants fled to places of safety as earth continued to tremble.

Jucuarán, Usulután. P: 1,205. From Usulután 40 km south-east. F: Candelaria, fair Jan. 20-Feb. 2; Santa Ana, Jul. 23-24.

Situated on the slopes of the mountain of the same name, eight kilometers from the Pacific Ocean, and therefore open to invasions of pirates. Large forests wherein are medicinal plants, construction and furniture woods. Name means "Hill of the warring ants."

Jutiapa, Cabañas. P: 1,050. From Sensuntepeque 47 km west. F: San Cristóbal, Nov. 20-21; La Cruz, May 2-3.

Situated at the foot of El Platanar mountain. Pre-Columbian village formerly had only Indian inhabitants. Name means "River of the jute" (mollusc exuding a dark dye). On pre-Columbian site in region of Tepeahua on the hill of Azacualpa. The population moved because the effigy of San Cristóbal appeared at the foot of a large tree with white flowers; this was interpreted by the Dominican missionaries as indicating that on that spot should be erected a church.

La Libertad, La Libertad. P: 1,950. From Santa Tecla 28 km south; 36 km from San Salvador. F: Concepción, Dec. 1-8.

On the Pacific Ocean, having a solid iron wharf built in 1867. The port was first opened in 1824. Situated between Peña Partida and Chilama. Many week-end residences of Capital socialites who swim at Obispo Beach and Conchalía Beach. The roadstead is called *Tepeagua.* Two kilometers distant is estuary of Tepeagua with an island having a deep cave. Nearby is River Comasagua, also small River Conchaliyito. The tides have a three-hour interval.

La Unión, La Unión. E: 72 ft. P: 8,064. From San Salvador 249 km east. F: Virgen de Concepción, Dec. 12.

The newest and most up-to-date port of the country, the only one boasting a concrete wharf where ships may come

alongside at the suburb of Cutuco, the terminal of the
International Railway of Central America, situated in a
beautiful land-locked harbor. During the colonial period this
site (Cutuco) was called *Embarcadero de las Amapalas,* and
the site of La Unión was known as the village of San Carlos.
The port has a three-hour and fifteen-minute tide interval.
Port of entry for small vessels plying across the Bay of Fonseca, which anchor at the other wharf in La Unión village.
The port is united to the principal towns of this section by
splendid roads and by railroad to the rest of the country.

Meanguera de la Bahia or **del Golfo.** From La Unión 48
km south. F: San José, Mar. 17-19.

Discovered in the gulf of Fonseca in 1522 by pilot Andrés
Niño, who called it Petronila. Situated on an island in the
Bay of Fonseca. The 500 inhabitants repopulated this site
scarcely a century ago. The island is situated so that the
eastern part demarks the eastern boundary of the Republic
of El Salvador. The inhabitants fish and grow corn. Formerly
the island was known as Quetzaltepetl, later as Mangola;
from 1683 it was called Santa María Magdelena de Meanguera. Pirates and disease killed most of the inhabitants;
the survivors fled to a site of safety on the mainland early
in the sixteenth century. The Royal authorities decreed that
all the inhabitants should be evacuated and granted their
petition for lands to settle on the slopes of the Conchagua
Volcano and region of Joateca. Later they were transferred
again in 1680 to the present site, so that they might manage
the ferry canoes across the Torla River, that the commerce
between the provinces of Gracias and San Miguel might
be aided.

Before leaving the island the Spanish authorities ordered
the inhabitants to burn their cultivated plots of land and
huts, and to fill in the sweet water well on the island and
destroy everything that might help the pirates.

Mejapa, San Salvador. P: 2,130. From San Salvador 24 km
. north. F: San Jerónimo, Sept. 29-30.

Railroad communication. Nexapa or Guaymoco, situated
on the right bank of the River Sucio, was celebrating the
feast of San Jerónimo in 1658 when an earthquake and
enormous eruption of lava took place and the panic-stricken
inhabitants fled to safety carrying their saint with them. The
village was reconstructed on the present site. Nevertheless,
earthquakes and lava flows have been a menace. From the
railroad glimpses may be had of various lava beds: on the
right-hand side is one at least five hundred years old whereon
bits of vegetation have started, while others remain a sad-
looking mass. The name means "In the river of ashes."

Metapan (San Pedro), Santa Ana. P: 1,875. From Santa Ana
56 km north. F: San Pedro, Jun. 28-29; Los Santos, Oct.
28-Nov. 4; Señor de Ostua, Feb. 24.

Railroad communication. Region for sugarcane, coffee,
cereals, cattle ranches, sugar mills, and lime.

The first village on this site was populated by survivors
of a flood from Lake Güija, early in the seventeenth century.
Picturesque present old colonial town is near the river of
the same name, which overflows and has caused much havoc
in the town and undermined the abutment of the cathedral.
This church is the most beautiful surviving colonial building in the country; its architectural style has no Indian
adulteration. It has one high nave larger than usual, without columns. Rich artistic altar with silver decorations; the
silver mines in this region supplied the metal. Religious
paintings of interest, altar pieces incrusted with gold leaf
and carvings. Data for this church state it was built in 1743,
but this seems more in accordance with its reconstruction,
as its style denotes a much earlier period—toward the beginning of the baroque style of the seventeenth century.

The Calvary Church is of more simple construction; in it
are the famous Señor de Ostua and Señor de Angüe, the

former a black image resembling the Christ of Esquipulas, which was formerly housed in what are now the ruins of a colonial church in the destroyed village of Ostua, near Lake Güija, and which the terror-stricken survivors carried with them as they came to Metapán to settle and pray before their Señor de Ostua.

Name of town means "River of the Magüeyes." The inhabitants, especially the women, were very prominent in the movement for independence.

Nahuizalco, Sonsonate. E: 230 m. P. 6,039. From Sonsonate 8 km north. F: Rosario, Oct. 23-25; San Juan, Jun. 22-25.

Good roads. Indian mat and basket craft center. Situated in a valley at the foot of Loma Larga Hill. One legend states that the village was established by four families of Izalco Indians immediately after the Conquest. Hence name of place, meaning "Four Izalcos."

Nueva Esparta, La Unión. P: 3,000. From La Unión 80 km north. F: San Pedro, Jun. 28-30; Señor de las Misericordias, Sept. 13-15.

Situated in a valley between the hills of La Leona, La Peñona, and Piedra Alta. It was populated by people from Honduras, who came from Curarén in 1838, with the army of General Morazán; he called them his "courageous Spartans," hence the name of the present site. The former site near here was called Honduritas, but was destroyed by fire during one of the revolutions. The present site was definitely established in 1847.

Oloquilta, La Paz. E: 270 m. P: 2,880. From Zacatecoloca 50 km west. F: San Juan, Jun. 23-24; El Rosario, 2d Sunday in October; Caridad, Ash Wednesday, lasting until the next Sunday.

Region for coffee and cereals. Center for weaving palm leaf hats and baskets. Name means "Place of the painted

heart" or "Place of the thread worm," according to interpretation.

Pasaquina, La Unión. P: 1,366. From La Unión 42 km north.
F: San Sebastián, Jan. 19-20; Fair of La Ascención, also
called *Fiesta de Nuestra Señora de los Desamparados,* May
12-14; and El Salvador, Aug. 4-6.

Situated near the boundary with Honduras. The name is
a corruption of Paso de Quina (Quinine ferry) because this
village was a resting place for the pack trains of men and
mules that brought quinine from Honduras (Choluteca) to
San Salvador, from where it was reshipped in colonial times
to Guatemala and Mexico. After the Indians left this village,
it was occupied by *ladinos.* The church was built in 1615.
The town is established on the cool banks of the river of
the same name. Name means "Town of the white beans."

The enormous inverted rock balanced precariously on a
small stone in the suburb of San Eduardo is interesting. Also
of interest is the large grotto hidden by a forest on the Cerro
Mongote, which was a refuge for pirates who infested the
Gulf of Fonseca during the seventeenth and eighteenth centuries. This region is the center of salt works.

Puerto el Triunfo, Usulután, also called **Puerto del Triunfo
de los Libres.** P: 1,100. From Usulután 20 km southwest.

Situated on the Bay of Jiquilisco. Region of cattle
ranches, cereals, salt works, and fishing. No particular feast is
celebrated. Mentioned because at one time this port was
considered as a possibility for enlargement, to establish a
regular port of entrance to the country; though it has never
served as a port for any length of time, it is nevertheless
a good roadstead with conditions for sheltering vessels; has
twelve feet of water at low tide and twenty-two feet at high
tide.

Quelepa, San Miguel. P: 700. From San Miguel 8 km northwest. F: Apóstol Santiago, Jul. 25; Concepción, Jun. 7-8.

Village on banks of River San Esteban, or Moncagua. Name means "The broken fox" or "Stone jaguar." Pre-Columbian ruins as well as Lenca ruins are found between this village and Moncagua.

Quezaltepeque, La Libertad. E: 415 m. P: 6,193. From Santa Tecla 18 km north; from San Salvador 28 km northwest. F: Dec. 19, "titular" Fair, Dec. 15-27.

One mile distant is large La Toma swimming pool. Center for ceramic craft. Situated on northeast slope of San Salvador Volcano; nearby is the colonial bridge Atapasco over River Sucio. Six kilometers north is Carranchagua Mountain. Name means "Hill of the quetzal bird."

San Alejo, La Unión. P: 4,000. From La Unión 24 km northwest. F: Señor de los Milagros, Jan. 13-14; Candelaria, Jun. 24-25.

Formerly an Indian village with some *mulatos,* later superseded by *ladinos.* Birthplace of Dr. Rafael Zaldívar, ex-President of the Republic.

There are several villages by the name of **San Antonio: San Antonio** belonging to the jurisdiction of Ciudad Barrios, established in 1855; **San Antonio de los Ranchos,** established as a village in 1815 (a Dutch priest, Pedro Reynen, changed its name to **San Antonio Los Reyes** in 1870); **San Antonio Pajonal,** the newest of this name, established in 1945; **San Antonio Masahuat,** department of La Paz, is the best known. Its name means "The owners of deer"; an old establishment.

San Francisco Morazán or **San Francisco Gotera,** capital of the department of Morazán. E: 948 m. P: 2,950. From San Salvador 169 km east. F: San Francisco de Asís, Oct. 2-5;

El Rosario, Nov. 10-13; Pascua de Navidad, Dec. 23-24; Palm Sunday.

Formerly located at the top of the Coroban Hill, because of violent storms it was transferred to its present site on southwest slope of the same hill near the San Francisco River. Known as Gotera in colonial days, but changed to San Francisco in 1887, when it already had been granted the title "Ciudad." Region rich in sugarcane, cereals, fiber plants, indigo, and gold and silver mines. Two kilometers west of town are thermal springs having medicinal qualities. The cool springs, Agua Fría, provide water for the town. The present site was known formerly as *El Plan del Cacao* (The plain where cacao grows). *Gotera* means "Hill of the snakes."

There are several towns and villages by the name of **San Francisco** besides the one mentioned above: **San Francisco Chinameca,** site of pre-Columbian Pipil Indians; **San Francisco Javier,** a village established in 1932 when several hamlets formed this village; **San Francisco Menéndez,** and other minor ones.

San Isidro, Cabañas. P: 4,200. From Sensuntepeque 15 km west on the San Salvador highway. F: San Isidro, May 14-15; Concepción, 2d Sunday in November.

South of village is the Viejo River, with two high waterfalls. Region of gold and silver mines and lime deposits.

There are several places called **San Isidro, San Isidro Labrador** included.

San Juan Nonualco, La Paz. P: 5,500. From Zacatecoluca 3 km west. F: San Juan Bautista, Jun. 15-24; Romería de la Cruz, Apr. 22-May 3.

Ancient site. Located on a stony and broken terrain. Center for ceramic craft.

San Julian (Cacaluta), Sonsonate. E: 510 m. P: 1,825. From
Sonsonate 28 km southeast. F: San Julián Obispo, Jan. 24-28.

The Indian name *Cacaluta* means "Place of the crows."
Pre-Columbian establishment. Region for coffee, cereals, and
balsam. Cattle ranches.

San Martín, San Salvador. P: 2,210. From San Salvador 20 km
east. F: San Martín, Nov. 6-12.

Railroad station. Old village already known in 1705.
Granted the title "Villa" in 1896. During colonial days
known as San Martín Perulapán. Indian name *Polulupan*
means "River of the *polulos*," a fish. On this Pipil site in
1530, Captain Martín Estete, the Spaniard of historical fame,
established the town of Ciudad de los Caballeros.

San Miguel de la Frontera, formerly situated on the plains of
Poshotlan, capital of the department of San Miguel. E: 106
m. P: 27,013. From San Salvador 138 km east. F: Fair of
La Paz, Nov. 17-21; Romería de Santa Lucía renowned since
colonial days; Fair May 5-8.

Railroad and highway communication to the rest of the
country; the metropolis of the East and the third in importance in the country. Established in 1530 by Luis de
Moscoso, who carried out orders of Don Pedro de Alvarado;
conceded title "Ciudad" in 1586. Center of commercial
activities of this region, located on the former site of Chaparrestique. His Majesty the King of Spain granted this town
the title *Muy noble y muy leal Ciudad de San Miguel* on
July 15, 1812, because the inhabitants opposed independence.

The parish church has a renowned image of Nuestra
Señora de la Paz. Two convents: San Francisco, built in
1574, under the name of Vera Cruz, and later called San
Francisco; the other, Nuestra Señora de la Merced, in 1630.
The Bishop of San Miguel has great influence in all this

region and resides in the Bishop's Palace. The Cathedral has low towers and probably belongs to eighteenth-century architecture, similar to the church of La Asunción at Izalco, and both are like the Cathedral at León in Nicaragua, so it is probable that the same colonial architect designed them all. In 1655 a volcanic catastrophe destroyed most of the town; it is said that in the church only the image of Lucifer remained intact because even the sculptured wood of that effigy was refused by the fire. That of San Francisco de Asís was left intact in the San Francisco church. After earthquakes and fire had wrought havoc, tributes were annulled by order of the *Real Audiencia* in 1655 so that the Indians could be induced to work in reconstructing the town.

During the colonial era this town was important, and the present town still has a colonial imprint, with its large houses and the even tenor of its life. It has beautiful parks with flowers of many kinds, good schools, a newspaper, hospital, and a very active commerce. However, in 1693 earthquakes destroyed the greater part of the town, but it has been reconstructed according to its former architecture. It is the center of a region rich in cereals, sugarcane, coffee, indigo, tobacco, and fiber-producing henequen. It is the birthplace of many men prominent in the history of this country: Juan J. Cañas, author of the national anthem; Dr. José Antonio Rosales, whose statue is in front of the radio station in this town; Francisco Antonio Gavidia, the outstanding poet and writer, and several others. The climate is warm. The Quelepa ruins are located in this region. A picturesque lagoon called Aramuaca is located twelve kilometers east of the town.

The British pirates in 1683, after being ousted from the coast, left behind in the port of Amapala (now extinct) an image of the Virgen de la Paz that was brought to this city, and the city was placed under her patronage.

Other villages by the name of **San Miguel** are **San Miguel de las Mercedes, San Miguel Tepezontes.**

San Pedro Masahuat, La Paz. P: 2,400. From Zacatecoluca 28
km northwest. F: San Pedro, Jun. 25-29. Fair: El Señor de
Esquipulas, Jan. 11-15.

Old village. Center for weaving palm leaf hats. Region
for coffee, cereals, indigo, and cattle ranches.

San Pedro Nonualco, La Paz. P: 4,625. From Zacatecoluca 20
km north-northwest. F: San Pedro, Jun. 26-29. Fair, Nombre
de Jesús, Feb. 1-15.

Established by *ladinos* who fled from the depredations of
the Indian Aquino. Large village. Church has nicely carved
pulpit. In 1936 the gold and silver cimboriums were stolen
from the church. The angry villagers gathered for a large
pilgrimage and were joined by people from all over the
country to fast and pray that the sacred relics might be recovered. The wafers were lost and word spread that the
thief ate them and thus became invisible when he hid in
the ravine where the sacred vessels were later recovered.
The Calvary Church at entrance to village is located in a
picturesque spot, high on the slopes of a hill.

This place is a commercial center and Saturday market
is well attended; simple textiles from San Sebastian, ceramics
from San Juan Nonualco, tobacco from Verapa, black sugar
and henequen from San Miguel, and corn from nearby
regions are attractively displayed. Streets are lined with
orange trees, and there are splendid views of the distant
Volcano Izalco, Cerro de las Pavas in Cojutepeque, and the
valley of Jiboa.

During the fair typical dances are staged with music produced by Indian instruments. The famous *Dos Niños Dioses*
from Cojutepeque arrive for the festivities, that is to say,
two images of the Christ Child are brought with great ceremony; one has black eyes and black hair. The other, called
El Niño Sarco, has blue eyes and fair hair. The latter, wherever it passes on its way, is received with money and gifts,
and it is a privilege to house the Niño Sarco. Usually this

is granted to the majordomo of the feast. During one of the dances, this white Christ is brought out covered with a veil, while typical dances are performed around it. Though the priests have tried to suppress this performance and forcibly take the two images to the church, they have not been able to accomplish it to date. Typical of these feasts is a sweetmeat called *chancacas,* a candy in the form of a dove, made of ground corn and sugar; the young men at the feast must present the girls of their choice with some of these. North of town is the River Atimiaya. Nonualco means "Place of the Nonuales," because a branch of the Nonuales Indians was located on this site.

San Pedro Perulapan, Cuzcatlán. E: 200 m. P: 1,100. From Cojutepeque 18 km northwest. F: San Pedro, Jun. 28-29.

West of the town is famous hill with the bell tower where a battle was fought between the forces of the Honduras General Ferrera and the Salvadoreans commanded by General Morazán, who vanquished the former in 1839. The village was established in the middle of the sixteenth century and granted the title "Villa" in 1590, and that of town in 1921.

San Rafael Cedros, Cuzcatlán. P: 1,500. From Cojutepeque 8 km east. F: San Pablo, Jun. 28-30; Fair, San Rafael, Nov. 27.

Located in a valley between Las Delicias and Nancintepeque hills, on the highway between Cojutepeque and San Vicente. Formerly known only as El Cedro or as San Rafael Arcangel.

Several other places are called **San Rafael: San Rafael de Oriente,** formerly called El Tempiscal; **San Rafael Obrajuelo,** named in honor of ex-president Dr. Rafael Zaldivar.

San Vicente, capital of the department of San Vicente. P: 10,019. From San Salvador 60 km east. F: San Vicente Abad, the Patron Saint, Dec. 19-26; De los Santos, Nov. 1-2.

Town located in the valley of Acahuapa at the foot of Chinchontepec or San Vicente Volcano. Good water supplied by the Agua Caliente River. On railroad.

This region was the habitat of Spanish families living on sugar plantations and working in indigo factories. They lived in constant fear of the Negroes and Indians who worked on the plantations. On December 26, 1635, fifteen of the principal Spanish families who had petitioned for this site gathered under the shade of a large *tempisque* tree (the same tree is still standing in the town), and for mutual protection established this Spanish town, naming it San Vicente de Lorenzana and placing it under the protection of Don Alvaro Quiñonez y Osorio, Marqués de Lorenzana, Captain General and Governor of the Kingdom of Guatemala, a descendant of the House of San Vicente de Abad, one of the noblest of Spain; they dedicated the village to San Vicente de Ferrer. The Governor General helped in every way to further the interests of the town. He died in a storm at sea, having built for himself a tomb that remains empty in the chapel of La Virgen del Socorro in the Cathedral of La Muy Noble y Muy Leal Ciudad de Santiago de los Caballeros (now Antigua Guatemala).

This lush valley belonged to the Indians of Apastepeque. Many other Spanish families joined the settlers. One of the first was Don Alonso Vides de Alvarado, a direct descendant of Gonzalo de Alvarado, brother of Don Pedro, the conqueror. The title "Villa San Vicente de Austria" was granted by His Majesty King Philip IV, previous to a gift of 1,600 pesos in gold, and the Real Audiencia in Guatemala signed the grant in 1658.

In 1812 the Cortes Generales granted the town the title "Ciudad," in the name of the Regency of the Kingdom.

The town has been destroyed several times by earthquakes. The last time was on December 19, 1936; it further ruined some of the few colonial buildings in the country. Some of the church edifices still give an idea of their past splendor. The Iglesia Parroqual facing the park was built in 1546; it had a seventeenth-century silver altarpiece, other church ornaments of silver, and very old images, such as *El Niño de Jesús de Praga*. El Pilar Church was the best and most artistic building in the country, probably designed by the same architect who designed the small church of Nuestra Señora de Pilar in Sonsonate, in what might be called American colonial baroque style: the straight line is preserved with a low roof structure over three naves separated by rhomboid pillars, and profusely decorated according to eighteenth-century style. This church was started in 1762; in its catacombs are buried the famous fathers of their country, Don José Simeón and Don Antonio José Cañas (1785), a descendant of the principal Spanish family that established this town.

The clock of the Parroquia was donated in 1772 by Presbítero Dr. Manuel Antonio Molina y Cañas, belonging to the noble lineage of Doña Isabel de Alvarado, daughter of Don Jorge, the conqueror. He was also one of the principal conspirators for the movement of independence, though he refused to join the movement of the fifth of November of 1811. As a member of the *Deputación Provincial* he signed the declaration of Central American independence. He is buried in the Cathedral in Guatemala City. The Santuario Church, situated a few steps away from the traditional *tempisque* tree, is of a severe colonial type of architecture. The Calvario Church was destroyed, and the present edifice was built in 1784.

Several of the old colonial patriarchal houses have been reconstructed, such as a corner house near Central Park known as "Casa de los Miranda"; it has windows protected by iron bars and symbolic double-headed eagles of the Royal House of Spain under Charles V.

Located on the Pan American Highway and center of a fertile valley, San Vicente is an active market center. The Sunday market is well attended; traders arrive from San Antonio Masahuat with palm leaf hats; shrimp come from the Pacific Coast, corn and other articles from far-off regions.

In 1782 San Vicente was the center of the indigo cultivation, and this plant is still the most famous of its kind in

Central America. A treatise on the subject of indigo was written by a Franciscan friar, Juan de Dios Cid, a very renowned pamphlet titled *El Puntero Apuntador con Apuntes Breves*. In 1782 this place was chosen to establish a Montepío and the famous *Sociedad de Cosecheros de Añil* (Society of Indigo Growers); the indigo fair hitherto held in Apastepeque was transferred here and was celebrated at the end of that year by the largest and best-attended fair ever held in the whole Kingdom. This indigo fair was transferred to San Salvador City in 1784, but as it was not successful in that city it was later reinstated at Apastepeque.

San Vicente was the capital of the Republic from 1834 to 1839. It has been known for the many illustrious persons born here: one was Ana Guerra de Jesús, 1639, a saintly woman known for her charities. She later moved to the capital of Guatemala and was buried in the Jesuit church of that city under the principal altar (Antigua).

The dance "Flores de Mayo" is performed here in honor of the Virgin Mary. The procession wends its way through the streets of the town; children escort the figure and throw flowers, corn, and candy in its path.

Santa Ana, or **Cihuatethuacan** (Town of the Priestess), capital of the department of Santa Ana. P: 52,568. From San Salvador 66 km west. F: Santa Ana, Jul. 17-26 (fiestas Julias); Patron Saint, La Virgen del Rosario, whose feast is in October.

Located in a valley on the northeast slope of the volcano Ilamatepec or Santa Ana; an old settlement mentioned in history in 1576, granted the title "Villa" in 1812, and that of "Ciudad" in 1824.

Splendid region for agriculture with many large estates with good houses and large coffee production. Region is also rich in sugarcane, cereals, and cattle ranches. Largest coffee mill in the world is on the outskirts of the city. This second largest city of the Republic has colonial-style houses, paved streets, good schools, a public library, national theater, movie houses, art and normal schools, hospital, orphanage, children's hospital, Cathedral, hotels, clubs, newspapers.

The Cathedral is one of the finest buildings in the country in Spanish Gothic style, with images by famous sculptors; the El Calvario is of the colonial style of architecture. Well-attended churches are the Virgen del Carmen and San Lorenzo.

Parque Anita Alvarado was named in honor of a child of that name who at the risk of her life saved her brothers and sisters from a fire.

The See of Santa Ana has a Bishop who resides near the Cathedral. Famous feasts and a fair during July attract merchants and others from Mexico, Guatemala, Honduras, and Nicaragua. The yearly expositions are a good sample of the arts and crafts of the country. This city is the center of the Western Military Zone. A high peak east of the city is Cerro Redondo. A sweetmeat, *Cajeta de Santa Ana,* made with almonds and candied fruit, has become famous. This place was already known as Santa Ana in 1576, though mentioned in history as Santa Ana Grande. In 1822 Santa Ana pronounced herself in favor of the ephemeral Empire of Agustín Iturbide. In 1780 the inhabitants helped to oust the British from the island of Roatain.

Santa Catarina Masahuat, Sonsonate. P: 1,870. From Juayua 8 km south. F: Santa Catarina, Nov. 20-25.

Indians of Nahuatl descent live here. Name *Masahuat* means "River belonging to the deer owners" or "Weed of the deer." Region for cereals, mat weaving craft. Nearby waterfall, Yuhualco, forms a cool bathing pool, Pozo de Cantería. Four kilometers north is a large waterfall formerly known as El Coyote, now named Buena Vista, formed by the River Tepechapa.

Santa María Ostuma, La Paz. P: 1,725. From Zacatecoloca 15 km northwest. F: Nuestra Señora de Candelaria, Jan. 28-

Feb. 3. From then on the feast continues in the neighboring village of San Pedro Nonualco.

ᴧ Formerly village of Indians, now of *ladinos*. Located on the southwest slope of the Chichontepec volcano. Colonial church in the style of Churiguerra, with famous Virgen de Candelaria. Legend states that the Indians moved over to San Pedro Nonualco and took with them this Virgin to place in their church. A few days later the Virgin was back in her own church in this village, having wet feet, because she had passed through the torrent at the bottom of the deep ravine separating the two villages. The Virgin stayed here, taken over to the other village during the fair. El Calvario is a smaller church. Indian name of village means "Place of the skunks" (Ostuacán). The pineapples of this region are considered the best in the country.

Santiago María, Usulután. E: 660 m. P: 5,900. From Usulután 24 km northwest. F: San Rafael, Nov. 1-5; Santiago Apóstol, Fair, Jul. 20-25.

Located on southeast slope of the Oromontique Mountain. Established as a town in 1874, very active commercially in agriculture: coffee, tobacco, wheat, and sugarcane. This place was known formerly as Alegría. It was much affected by earthquakes in 1951. Slowly the work of reconstruction started; now it has recovered from its severe losses.

Santiago Nonualco, La Paz. P: 3,680. From Zacatecoluca 9 km west. F: Santiago, Jul. 20-25.

Ancient establishment. Population rose against Indian Aquino, who had had himself crowned as "King of the Nonualcos." North of village is hill Agulteguya, with rich iron deposits.

Sensuntepeque, Cabañas. E: 700 m. P: 3,825. From San Salvador 89 km east-northeast. F: Fair, Santa Bárbara, Nov. 25-Dec. 8; El Tránsito, Aug. 8-15.

Formerly active indigo center. Region for sugarcane, coffee, cereals, and cattle, famous cheeses. Good ceramics. Legend states that the big hill has buried treasures of Indian chiefs. The Indians built a dam to let the waters of the nearby river flow over the entrance of the cave where the treasure is hidden, so that the conquerors would not find it. It consists of life-size gold figures of animals. Waters of the river are auriferous. The last descendant of the chiefs stated that he could not go to his rest leaving in his own possession the documents showing the location of the treasure, so he sent word to an Indian friend in Guatemala, where the documents were. However, these were later divided into small parts among descendants, and several were lost.

There is a good bathing beach by the River Lempa. The name Sensuntepeque or Centzuntli-Tepec means "Many mountains" or "Large hills."

Sesori, San Miguel. P: 1,000. From San Miguel 48 km northwest. F: Corazón de Jesús, Mar. 1-8; Fair, Sept. 15-22.

Nearby cattle ranch Espiritu Santo was site of the famous battle in April, 1839, between General Morazán and forces from Honduras and Nicaragua. Lime is mined. In 1563 the Lenca Indians still worshiped the deity Icelaca, who had the double privilege of predicting the past and the future.

Sociedad (Villa de), Morazán. P: 1,000. From San Francisco 16 km southeast. F: San Juan Bautista, Jun. 22-25; San Rafael, Dec. 3-4.

Gold and silver mines. Ex-president Braulio Carrillo of Costa Rica was assassinated in 1845 in a suburb of this village, which since then has been known as Portillo de Carrillo.

Sonsonate, capital of the department of Sonsonate, also called **Zonzonate,** or **Cenzontlat,** or **La Villa de la Santísima Trinidad de Sonsonate** by the Spanish conquerors. E: 223

m. P: 18,152. From San Salvador 65 km west. F: Nuestra
Señora de Candelaria, Jan. 20-Feb. 5; Jubileo de San
Antonio del Monte; Holy Week. The city is often called
Ciudad de las Palmeras (Town of the palms). Other feasts
are Dec. 24-25 and the movable feast of La Santísima Trini-
dad.

After Don Pedro de Alvarado conquered this region in
1524, a small village was established by the Spaniards, which
grew in importance. In 1552 the Oidor Licenciado Pedro
Ramírez de Quinónez was instructed by the *Real Audiencia
de Guatemala* to establish a village with five-hundred Spanish
families on the site of a valley with clear river waters and
many brooks, not far from the Indian region of Los Izalcos.
The name *Sonsonate* is derived from Sunzunat: a thousand
rivers. It was an important center during the colonial era,
because this valley produced an excellent quality of cocoa
bean. Churches and convents were erected. The four principal convents were those of Nuestra Señora de la Merced,
Santo Domingo, San Francisco called La Concepción (one
of the oldest, established in 1574), and San Juan de Dios.
The Santo Domingo Church was started in 1553, and the
permanent building erected in 1574. The Bishop of Guatemala, Fray Juan Zapata y Sandoval, was instrumental in
building it. Half a century later it was destroyed by earthquakes. Other churches: the Parroquial, which is large and
imposing, having seventeen cupolas of all sizes; the church
of Nuestra Señora del Pilar in colonial baroque style; the
hermitage of La Vera Cruz, El Angel on the outskirts of
town; and last, but not least, the colonial structure of San
Antonio on a hill near town, which is a famed place of Christian pilgrimage.

Fray Bernardino Pérez established the convent of Las
Beatas in 1774 as the nuns did not have any place of refuge
while repairing their convent after it was ruined in 1680.
It is difficult to fix exactly the various dates in this town because, unfortunately, the archives were burned in the sixteenth
century.

The dance and ceremony of *La Vela de la Vara* takes place in the suburb of Vera Cruz on the night before the *Alcalde* (the Mayor) takes the solemn oath of office for the coming year.

The modern town has attractive gardens, a municipal palace, colonial-style houses, a hospital, a very warm climate, and is most active commercially. Near are the hot springs which converge into the Rio Caliente; a swimming tank and waterfall are surrounded by beautiful scenery. The Nahuilingo Springs issue from the Izalco Volcano in the background. One kilometer northeast are the waterfalls of Bululú. The River Grande or Sensunapán passes through the middle of the town and forms this last-mentioned waterfall. It is this waterfall which provides the electric power for the town.

This town is the center for a rich region of agriculture and crafts, such as rope, mats, palm leaf hats, carved gourds, and baskets. This region, being rich, was populated from the time of the colony; the Spaniards, realizing the wealth, decided to divide the province of San Salvador or Cuzcatlán into three political jurisdictions, of which La Trinidad de Sonsonate was one, San Salvador and la Villa de San Miguel the others. The Constituent Assembly of the *Estados Centros Americanos* in 1824 conceded to the village the title "Ciudad" because of its importance.

The 5,000-foot Cerro Verde in the department of Sonsonate is a most attractive spot. On its summit a hotel has been built to view not only the spectacular eruptions of Izalco Volcano, but also to enjoy the delightful climate at this elevation.

Suchitoto, Cuzcatlán. E: 500 m. P: 10,315. From Cojutepeque 50 km northwest. F: Concepción and Santa Lucía, Dec. 6-13.

Located on the slopes of the Guazapa Volcano, this is one of the oldest establishments in the country. The former site, called Pueblo Viejo, was in Los Almendros, supposedly one of the sites where the primitive capital of the country was located. Suchitoto was granted the title "Villa" in 1836, and that of "Ciudad" in 1858. It was the capital of the department from 1835 to 1863. The name means "Bird flower" or "Choice bird." Birthplace of several presidents: Alfonso Quiñonez Malina, Pío Romero Bosque, and Arturo Araujo.

Tejutepeque, Cabañas. P: 1,250. From Sensuntepeque 43 km west. F: San Rafael Arcangel, Nov. 20-21; El Tránsito, Aug. 14-15.

Neighboring blue mineral earth used for coloring clay has given the name *Hill of the Texutli* (blue pigment). Near is the Barranca del Burro (Donkey ravine), a natural phenomenon worth seeing.

Tejutla (Santo Tomás), Chalatenango. P: 1,500. From Chalatenango 36 km west-northwest on the highway to Ocotepeque in Honduras. F: Santo Tomás, Dec. 20-25.

Cerro Torcido nearby is a hill with a deep crevice about which popular legends have been created. Tejutla is stated as established in the fifth century by tribes of Chorti Indians belonging to the Maya. The name is Ut-kajkta. It was originally a village on top of Cerro Negro.

Teotepeque, La Libertad. P: 1,680. From Santa Tecla 56 km southwest. F: Feb. 8-10; Concepción, Dec. 8.

Famous for the yearly pilgrimages to the shrine of Santa Ursula, the Patron Saint of the village of Jicalapa, built on a rock overlooking the sea three miles distant. The image of Santa Ursula was discovered in a cave on the seashore. Thousands gather to worship and celebrate during the feasts preceding February 8. The people join those of Masahuat to make a yearly pilgrimage to the village of Yayantique. The name *Teotepeque* means "Hill of God" or "Hill of devotion," probably because of a pre-Columbian shrine that was located there.

Texistepeque, Santa Ana. E: 558 m. P: 1,000. From Santa Ana 20 km northwest. F: Belén, Dec. 24-27; Señor de Esquipulas, Jan. 15.

The junction of railroad lines to San Salvador and Santa Ana on the International Railway of Central America; en route from Guatemala. Name means "Hill of the snail" or "Hill where stones are seen," according to different interpretations.

Tonacatepeque, San Salvador. P: 3,770. From San Salvador 17 km northeast. F: Fair, San Nicolás, Dec. 2-7. Famous pilgrimage during these festivities since 1792.

Birthplace of the famous worker for independence, Father Nicolás Aguilar. The name means "Country of the mountain deity."

Usulután, capital of the department of Usulután. F: Fair de Jesús, Jan. 12-15; Candelaria, Jan. 31-Feb. 2; Santa Catalina, Nov. 21-25.

On the south slope of the volcano of the same name and capital of the department of Usulután since 1865. The name means "Place of the ocelots." Region for agriculture, cattle ranges, and salt deposits. Nearby El Molino River has two waterfalls forming swimming pools.

Verapaz (Villa de), San Vicente. P: 1,700. From San Vicente 12 km west. F: San José, Mar. 18-19.

Located in the center of the valley of Jiboa, one of the most picturesque in the country. In 1913 the village was flooded by a current of mud and water.

Yayantique (San Juan), La Unión. E: 200 m. P: 1,200. From La Unión 36 km northwest. F: Candelaria, Jan. 31-Feb. 2; San Juan, June 24-25.

Nearby silver and coal mines. Forest abounds in dye plants: *Palo de Mashaste, Brasil, Nacascolo,* etc. Mat and hat weaving crafts, cool climate. Good hunting in the woods. Located on the slopes of the hill of the same name. Name means "Habitat of the rabbits" or "Hill of the Capulín" (a cherry-like fruit). It is a pre-Columbian Lenca site.

Zacatecoluca, capital of the department of La Paz. E: 172 m. P: 9,295. From San Salvador 72 km southeast on good highway, and 58 km by railway. F: Santa Lucía, Dec. 10-28; Fair de los Pobres during the same days of the feast.

Established early in the eighteenth century, given the title "Villa" in 1823, and that of *Generosa y Leal Ciudad* in 1843, and named as capital of the department in 1852. Birthplace of the priest José Simeón Cañas y Villacorta, the Central American slave liberator. Name means "Place of the owls."

BIBLIOGRAPHY

English

1. Biología Centrali-Americana. Aves. Vol. III
   Osbert Salvin and Frederick Ducane Godman: 1897-1904
2. Biología Centrali-Americana. Reptilia and Batrachia
   Albert C. L. B. Günther: 1885-1902
3. Excavations at Tajumulco, Guatemala
   Bertha P. Dutton and Hulda R. Hobbs: The University of
   New México Press, 1943
4. Notes on the Archaeology of Salvador
   Herbert J. Spinden: Reprinted from the American Anthro-
   pologist (N. S.) Vol. 17, No. 3, July-September, 1915
5. The States of Central America
   E. G. Squier: New York, Harper & Brothers, Publishers,
   1858
6. Carnegie Institution of Washington: Contributions to American Anthropology and History. Vol. IX, No. 44, 117. 1948

Spanish

1. Biografía de Vicentinos Ilustres, published by the Academia
   Salvadoreña de la Historia, 1935
2. Crónica de la Provincia del Santísimo Nombre de Jesús de
   Guatemala, R. P. Fr. Francisco Vázquez: Guatemala, edición Biblioteca Goathemala, 1940-1944
3. Flora Salvadoreña
   Dr. David J. Guzmán: San Salvador, El Salvador
4. Flora Salvadoreña
   Felix Choussey: Four Volumes. A publication of the Salvadorean Government, published in Switzerland
5. Historia General de las Indias Occidentales, y Particular de
   la Gobernación de Chiapa y Guatemala. Fray Antonio de
   Remesal: edición Biblioteca Goathemala, 1932

6. Historia de la Literatura de Centro América
   Leonardo Montalván: Tipografía Nacional, El Salvador, 1931
7. Masferrer Humorista
   José María Peralta Lagos: San Salvador, El Salvador, 1933
8. La Audiencia de Guatemala
   Antonio Vásquez de Espinosa: 1629, Guatemala, 1943
9. La Población de El Salvador
   Rodolfo Barón Castro: Publicado por el Consejo Superior de Investigaciones Científicas. Instituto Gonzalo Fernández de Oviedo. Madrid, 1942
10. Libro de Actas del Ayuntamiento de la Ciudad de Guatemala, publicado por el Museo de Guatemala, Guatemala 1856
11. Historia de la Provincia de San Vicente de Chiapas y Guatemala. Fray Francisco Ximenez: Biblioteca Goathemala, Guatemala, 1930
12. Orígenes de San Salvador, Cuzcatlán
    Jorge Lardé: San Salvador
13. Diccionario Geográfico de la República de El Salvador, América Central. Publicationes del Ministerio de Hacienda, Editado por la Dirección General de Estadística, 1940
14. Prontuario Geográfico—Comercial, Estadístico y Servicios Administrativos de El Salvador
    General José Tomás Calderón: San Salvador, 1932
15. Publicaciones del Ministerio de Hacienda (Editado por Dirección General de Estadística), San Salvador, El Salvador, 1930-1940
16. Recuerdos Salvadoreños
    Dr. José Antonio Cevallos: Imprenta Nacional, San Salvador, 1920
17. Revista del Ateneo de El Salvador
    publicado por El Ateneo, 1940 y siguientes números
18. Revista del Departamento de Historia
    Publicación del Ministerio de Instrucción Pública, San Salvador, Octobre 1929, Marzo 1930
19. Toponimia Arcaica de El Salvador
    Tomás Fidias Jiménez: publicado en El Salvador
20. La República de El Salvador
    editado por la Dirección General de Estadística de El Salvador bajo la dirreción de don Pedro S. Fonseca

21. Bosquejo Histórico de las Revoluciones de Centro América, 1811-1834. Alejandro Marure: tipografía de El Progreso, Guatemala, 1877

22. Datos para la Historia de Centro America relativos a la Unión de las Repúblicas del Istmo
    Pedro S. Fonseca: Guatemala, Tipografía La Independencia, 1912

23. Historia de El Salvador
    Dr. Santiago I. Barberena: San Salvador, Imprenta Nacional, 1914
    (dos volúmenes)

24. Idioma Pipil o Nahuat de Cuzcatlán y Tunalán
    Tomás Fidias Jiménez: Tipografía La Unión, San Salvador, 1937

25. Nociones de Historia de Centro América (Especial de El Salvador)
    Dr. Manuel Vidal: San Salvador, 1935

26. Documentos relativos a los Movimientos de Independencia en el Reino de Guatemala
    Leon Fermández: El Salvador, 1929

27. Aquino
    S. Calderón Ramírez: San Salvador, 1930

28. Compendio de Historia de la América Central
    Agustín Gómez Carrillo: Guatemala, 1906

29. Cuzcatlán Típico (dos volúmenes)
    María de Baratta: 1952, San Salvador, El Salvador

30. Diccionario Biográfico de El Salvador 1937
    Artículos por Braulio Perez Marchante

31. Sucinta Historia de los Municipios Salvadoreños
    Por Jorge Lardé y Larín. Director: Anales del Museo Nacional
    "David J. Guzman," San Salvador Cuzcatlán, Rep. de El Salvador (Varios artículos del mismo. Jorge Lardé y Larín en tomos 1 y 2 de los anales del Museo Nacional)

32. Descripción, Geografia y Estadistica de la Republica de El Salvador
    Doctor don Santiago I. Barberena: 1892

1. Estatutos de la distribución geografica de las razas indigenas de Mexico y Centro America por Dr. Santiago Barbercua en Repertorio Salvadoriño

2. Gramatica del Popoluca y del Chiquimulteco del Norte por
   E. Calderón 1892
3. Historia del Arte de la Musica de El Salvador por:
   Dr. Rafael Gonzalez Sol. 1945
4. Libro de Matimaticas por J. Perez de Moya. Impreso en casa
   de Juan Gracián. 1573

German

1. Indiana II, Mythen in der Muttersprache der Pipil von
   Izalco in El Salvador
   Leonhard Schultze: Jena, 1935
2. Ueber den Ursprung der Mittelamerikanische Kulturen.
   Eduard Seler: Berlin, 1902
3. Zur Ethnologie und Ethnographie des Nordlichen Mittel-
   amerika.
   Franz Termer: 1930

INDEX